Top 100 Most Delicious

Samosa Recipes

A Samosa Cookbook

by Graham Bourdain

Copyright Page

Top 100 Most Delicious Samosa Recipes

Copyright © 2023 by Graham Bourdain

First Edition

ISBN: 979-8-8690-2546-3

Disclaimer

The information in "Top 100 Most Delicious Samosa Recipes" is for general information purposes only. The author and publisher make no representation or warranties with respect to the accuracy, applicability, fitness, or completeness of the contents of this book. They disclaim any warranties (expressed or implied), merchantability, or fitness for any particular purpose.

The author and publisher shall in no event be held liable for any loss or other damages, including but not limited to special, incidental, consequential, or other damages. As always, the advice of a competent legal, tax, accounting, or other professional should be sought.

The author and publisher do not warrant the performance, effectiveness, or applicability of any sites listed or linked to in this book. All links are for information purposes only and are not warranted for content, accuracy, or any other implied or explicit purpose.

Note: Cooking times and temperatures, ingredient measurements, and instructions mentioned in this book are guidelines only. Variances in cooking appliances, altitudes, climates, and individual techniques may necessitate adjustments in preparation. Always use your best judgment and test recipes in small batches where possible.

Table of Contents

Seafood Samosas

Cheese-based Samosas

Breakfast Samosas

Sweet Samosas

Fusion Samosas

Vegan Samosas

Gluten-free Samosas

Exotic Samosas

1. Potato and Pea Samosas

Ah, the classic Potato & Pea Samosas. Takes me back to the bustling streets of Mumbai. It's more than just food, it's an experience. Every bite is a journey, with the crispy crust acting as the road and the savory filling as the vibrant scenes along the way.

Prep: 20 min. Cook: 30 min. Ready in: 50 min. Servings: 4

Ingredients:

All-purpose flour (maida) - 2 cups

Ghee or melted butter - 4 tbsp

Salt - 1/2 tsp

Potatoes, peeled and diced - 2 large

Green peas, boiled - 1 cup

Cumin seeds - 1 tsp

Ginger-garlic paste - 1 tsp

Green chilies, finely chopped - 2

Red chili powder - 1/2 tsp

Turmeric powder - 1/4 tsp

Garam masala - 1/2 tsp

Fresh coriander leaves, chopped - 1/4 cup

Oil for deep frying

Cooking Directions:

Alright folks, start off by taking that flour in a large bowl, throwing in the salt, and making a well in the center. Pour in that delightful, melted ghee or butter, whatever tickles your fancy. Now, gently knead it, adding water bit by bit, until you have a firm yet pliable dough. Once you're satisfied, cover it up with a cloth and let it take a short nap for about 30 minutes.

Meanwhile, let's get that filling going. Heat up a little oil in a pan. Throw in the cumin seeds. When they start dancing around, add the ginger-garlic paste, giving it a stir. Toss in those spicy green chilies and stir them until you get that heavenly aroma floating around your kitchen.

Time for the potatoes. Add 'em in. Give them a good mix, ensuring they're coated with all those flavors. Then, come the peas, red chili powder, turmeric, and garam masala. Let everything get to know each other in that pan for about 10 minutes on medium heat. Finish with the fresh coriander. Give it one final stir and set aside.

Back to our rested dough. Divide it into small balls, roll each one out, cut it in half, and shape into a cone. Stuff it with our delicious filling, seal the edges, and they're ready for a swim.

Heat up your oil for deep frying. Once hot, drop in the samosas, a few at a time. Fry until they're a gorgeous golden brown. Fish them out and place them on a paper towel to drain any excess oil.

And there you have it! A ticket to the streets of India, right in the palm of your hand. Best enjoyed with a tangy tamarind chutney and perhaps a cold beer. Here's to memories, flavors, and the simple joys of life.

Enjoy

2. Spinach and Paneer Samosas

Ah, the Spinach & Paneer Samosas. A twist on the classic, reminiscent of the palak paneer from the Punjabi dhabas. They're the kind of food that's like a comforting hug from an old friend.

Prep: 25 min. Cook: 30 min. Ready In: 55 min. Servings: 4

Ingredients:

All-purpose flour (maida) - 2 cups

Ghee or melted butter - 4 tbsp

Salt - 1/2 tsp

Fresh spinach, chopped - 2 cups

Paneer (Indian cottage cheese), crumbled - 1 cup

Onion, finely chopped - 1 medium

Green chilies, finely chopped - 2

Ginger-garlic paste - 1 tsp

Cumin seeds - 1/2 tsp

Garam masala - 1/2 tsp

Lemon juice - 1 tbsp

Fresh coriander leaves, chopped - 2 tbsp

Oil for frying and sautéing

Cooking Directions:

First things first, get that dough ready. In your trusty bowl, mix the flour and salt. Pour in the ghee or butter, and knead away, bit by bit, adding just enough water until you've got a firm ball of dough. Let it rest, snug under a cloth, for about 30 minutes.

Now, let's head north to Punjab with our filling. Heat a splash of oil in a pan. Toss in the cumin seeds and wait for them to splutter. Add the finely chopped onions, giving them a stir until they're translucent. Slide in the ginger-garlic paste, letting it infuse its magic with the onions. Add the green chilies and give it all a good stir.

Time for the spinach to join the party. Cook until it wilts and releases its water. Now, here's the star: the paneer. Mix it well with the spinach, adding the garam masala and the lemon juice to elevate the flavors. Cook for another 5 minutes and then sprinkle in that fresh coriander.

Back to the dough. Roll it out, cut in halves, shape them, stuff them, and seal them. Ready for the dive.

Heat up that oil. Once it's shimmering, carefully slide in the samosas, frying them till they turn a beautiful shade of golden brown. Once done, let them chill on a paper towel.

And voilà! A bite into these samosas is like diving straight into the heart of Punjab. Enjoy these beauties with some mint chutney and a side of spiced yogurt. Here's to culinary adventures and stories waiting to be told. Happy eating!

Enjoy

3. Mushroom and Corn Samosas

*Journeying onward, we find ourselves in the company of Mushroom
& Corn Samosas. Earthy mushrooms meeting the sweet notes of
corn; it's a culinary symphony. These pockets of joy are a testament
to the beauty of fusion in food.*

Prep: 20 min. Cook: 30 min. Ready in: 50 min. Servings: 4

Ingredients:

All-purpose flour (maida) - 2 cups

Ghee or melted butter - 3 tbsp

Salt - 1/2 tsp

Mushrooms, finely chopped - 1 cup

Sweet corn, boiled and coarsely mashed - 3/4 cup

Onion, finely chopped - 1 small

Garlic, minced - 2 cloves

Green chili, finely chopped - 1

Cumin seeds - 1/2 tsp

Black pepper, freshly ground - 1/4 tsp

Fresh coriander leaves, chopped - 2 tbsp

Oil for frying and sautéing

Cooking Directions:

Let's get down to business. Grab your flour, toss in that salt, and make a well. Into that goes your melted ghee or butter. Now, it's all hands-on deck, kneading until you've got a dough that's just right. Remember, it needs its beauty sleep, so cover and let it rest for 30 minutes.

As for the filling, start by heating a splash of oil in a pan. Drop in those cumin seeds, and when they start their little jig, add the onions. Saute them until they're golden and soft. Now, welcome the garlic and green chili to the mix, sautéing for another minute or two.

Mushrooms, your time has come. Into the pan they go. Let them cook down, releasing their moisture. Once that's mostly gone, it's the corn's turn to shine. Stir it in, add your seasonings – black pepper and salt. Mix it all up. Right before you take it off the heat, throw in the fresh coriander.

Now back to that dough. It's showtime. Roll, cut, shape, stuff, seal. You know the drill.

In a deep pan, heat up your oil. Once it's looking eager, slide in your samosas, letting them bask until they're a perfect golden hue. Lift them out, let them drip off any excess oil on some paper towels.

Here they are. Each bite is a walk in a forest with a sudden clearing revealing a cornfield. Best savored with a zesty lime chutney or perhaps a smooth avocado dip. Every meal is a story, and this one has a twist in every chapter.

Enjoy

4. Cauliflower and Broccoli Samosas

Alright, folks. Ever wonder what happens when the garden's two powerhouse veggies decide to party inside a crispy pocket? Introducing the Cauliflower & Broccoli Samosas. It's like a farmer's market rendezvous, right in your kitchen.

Prep: 25 min. Cook: 30 min. Ready in: 55 min. Servings: 4

Ingredients:

All-purpose flour (maida) - 2 cups

Ghee or melted butter - 3 tbsp

Salt - 1/2 tsp

Cauliflower, finely chopped - 1 cup

Broccoli, finely chopped - 1 cup

Onion, finely chopped - 1 small

Garlic, minced - 2 cloves

Ginger, minced - 1 inch piece

Green chili, finely chopped - 1

Turmeric powder - 1/4 tsp

Red chili powder - 1/4 tsp

Cumin seeds - 1/2 tsp

Coriander powder - 1/2 tsp

Fresh lemon juice - 1 tbsp

Oil for frying and sautéing

Cooking Directions:

Kick things off with the dough. In a bowl, whisk together the flour and salt. Now, drizzle in that golden ghee or butter. Dive in with your hands, kneading and adding water until the dough is just right. Once it's all together, cover it up and let it dream for about 30 minutes.

On to the main event. Warm up some oil in a skillet and let those cumin seeds have their moment to sizzle and pop. Slide in the onions and let them sweat and brown. Now, make some room for the ginger, garlic, and green chili to join the fiesta.

Here come the veggies. In goes the cauliflower and broccoli. Toss them around, letting them mingle and get to know all those spices. Sprinkle in the turmeric, red chili powder, and coriander powder. Give it a good mix, ensuring the veggies are coated and absorbing all that flavor.

Let it cook until the veggies are soft, yet still have a slight bite to them. Before wrapping things up, give it a splash of lemon juice for that zesty kick.

Time to circle back to the dough. Roll it, slice it, fill it, and seal those little pockets of joy.

Heat your frying vessel, get the oil bubbling, and gently nestle in the samosas. Fry until they're blushing golden, and then rescue them onto some paper towels.

And there you have it. A vegetable duet that's music to your taste buds. Dip them into a tangy tamarind sauce, or maybe even a cool cucumber yogurt dip. It's the symphony of flavors that makes the food journey so damn exciting. Cheers to more adventures on the plate!

Enjoy

5. Mixed Vegetable Samosas

So, you want a little bit of everything? I get that. Today's story is about the medley of flavors and textures, packed inside a crispy golden shell. Enter, the Mixed Vegetable Samosas. They're like the all-star band of the veggie world.

Prep: 30 min. Cook: 30 min. Ready In: 1 h. Servings: 4

Ingredients:

All-purpose flour (maida) - 2 cups

Ghee or melted butter - 3 tbsp

Salt - 1/2 tsp

Potatoes, boiled and mashed - 1/2 cup

Green beans, finely chopped - 1/4 cup

Carrots, finely chopped - 1/4 cup

Peas - 1/4 cup

Onion, finely chopped - 1 small

Ginger, minced - 1 inch piece

Green chili, finely chopped - 1

Cumin seeds - 1/2 tsp

Coriander powder - 1/2 tsp

Turmeric powder - 1/4 tsp

Garam masala - 1/4 tsp

Fresh coriander leaves, chopped - 2 tbsp

Oil for frying and sautéing

Cooking Directions:

Let's start with that dough. Mix your flour and salt in a bowl, then pour in that gorgeous ghee or butter. Now, get your hands in there and knead. Once you've got a nice, smooth dough, let it sit tight under a cloth for about 30 minutes.

For the heart of these samosas, heat a dollop of oil in a pan and drop in the cumin seeds. When they start dancing, welcome the onions, ginger, and green chili to the stage. Cook them until they're golden and smelling divine.

Next up, the veggie ensemble. Potatoes, beans, carrots, and peas, all jumping into the mix. Toss and turn, and let them get acquainted with their spicy companions: turmeric, coriander powder, and garam masala. Cook until everything's tender and the spices have serenaded the veggies.

Just before you pull it off the heat, a sprinkle of freshly chopped coriander. It's like the encore they didn't see coming.

Back to our dough. Roll it out, cut circles, and get ready to stuff. Once they're all filled and sealed, it's into the hot oil they go. Fry until they're golden, turning them occasionally for an even tan.

Voilà! Samosas fit for a feast. Every bite is like diving into a bustling street market, where each vendor (or in this case, vegetable) brings something unique to the table. Pour yourself a cold beer, or maybe a minty yogurt dip on the side, and savor the journey. After all, it's the mix of experiences that make life rich, isn't it?

Enjoy

6. Lentil and Spinach Samosas

Sometimes, the simplest of ingredients come together to form a gastronomic orchestra. Today, we're looking at two rock stars of the vegetarian world: lentils and spinach. Together in a samosa, they're a bit like a folk duo — earthy, soulful, and immensely satisfying.

Prep: 30 min. Cook: 35 min. Ready in: 1 h. 5 min. Servings: 4

Ingredients:

All-purpose flour (maida) - 2 cups

Ghee or melted butter - 3 tbsp

Salt - 1/2 tsp

Lentils (preferably green or brown), soaked and boiled - 1 cup

Spinach, finely chopped - 1 cup

Onion, finely chopped - 1 medium

Garlic, minced - 3 cloves

Ginger, minced - 1 inch piece

Green chili, chopped - 1

Cumin seeds - 1/2 tsp

Coriander powder - 1/2 tsp

Garam masala - 1/4 tsp

Lemon juice - 1 tbsp

Oil for frying and sautéing

Cooking Directions:

Begin the gig with the dough. In a spacious bowl, let the flour, salt, and that glorious ghee meet. Work them into a soft dough, adding water as you go. Once it's all harmonious, cover it up and let it rest for about 30 minutes.

Onto our dynamic duo. In a pan, heat some oil and toss in the cumin seeds. Wait for them to perform their opening act, then usher in the onions, garlic, ginger, and green chili. Let them groove together until the onions are golden.

Now, in with the lentils. These legumes have soaked, boiled, and are ready to party. Add them to the pan, followed by the finely chopped spinach. Shower the mix with coriander powder and garam masala. Let them mingle, groove, and become one. Once everything's nice and cooked, a splash of lemon juice to lift the mood.

Now, our rested dough is back in the limelight. Roll it out, slice it into the desired shape, and fill each with our lentil-spinach melody. Seal them up and get them ready for their final act.

Into the oil they go, frying until they're a perfect golden brown, crispy on the outside, soulful on the inside.

And there you have it — Lentil & Spinach Samosas. They're hearty, they're wholesome, and they're just waiting to be dunked into a tangy chutney or enjoyed with a side of spicy pickles. This is comfort food with a touch of elegance, a symphony in every bite.

Enjoy

7. Potato and Bell Pepper Samosas

Ever been to a lively salsa club? The energy, the colors, the beats? That's what these Potato & Bell Pepper Samosas feel like. A dance of vibrant colors and flavors, every bite is like a fiesta. Let's put on our dancing shoes, shall we?

Prep: 25 min. Cook: 30 min. Ready in: 55 min. Servings: 4

Ingredients:

All-purpose flour (maida) - 2 cups

Ghee or melted butter - 3 tbsp

Salt - 1/2 tsp

Potatoes, boiled and diced - 1 cup

Bell peppers (a mix of red, yellow, and green), finely chopped - 1 cup

Onion, finely chopped - 1 medium

Ginger, minced - 1 inch piece

Garlic, minced - 2 cloves

Green chili, chopped - 1

Cumin seeds - 1/2 tsp

Coriander powder - 1/2 tsp

Turmeric powder - 1/4 tsp

Garam masala - 1/4 tsp

Lemon juice - 1 tbsp

Oil for frying and sautéing

Cooking Directions:

Step one: the dance of the dough. Grab your flour, the salt, and a generous dollop of ghee. Mix and knead. It's a waltz of sorts, rhythmically adding water, pushing, and pulling until you have a soft, pliable dough. Let it take a break and rest for about 30 minutes.

Meanwhile, the fiesta filling. In a pan, throw in a splash of oil and your cumin seeds. Let them crackle like the claps of a flamenco. Introduce the onions, ginger, garlic, and green chili. Wait for them to dance around, turning a golden hue.

Time for the stars: potatoes and bell peppers. Slide them into the pan. It's a riot of colors, like a carnival. Sprinkle the coriander powder, turmeric, and garam masala. Dance and toss them around till everything's melded together. Just before bowing out, a zesty squeeze of lemon juice to tie it all up.

Back to our rested dough, it's showtime. Roll, cut, fill, and seal. The rhythm is important; you'll find yours.

Final act, the deep-fry. Into bubbling hot oil, they go, twirling and turning until golden and crisp.

"Step back and admire your handiwork — Potato & Bell Pepper Samosas, a medley of flavors and colors that promises a party in every bite. Grab a tangy tamarind dip or a spicy mint chutney, and let the fiesta continue.

Enjoy

8. Cottage Cheese and Corn Samosas

You know, in the world of culinary jazz, where ingredients improvise and play off each other, cottage cheese and corn are like two musicians finding a surprising, yet delightful harmony. Their duet is melodic, soothing, with just a touch of playfulness. Let's dive into this musical number, shall we?

Prep: 20 min. Cook: 35 min. Ready in: 55 min. Servings: 4

Ingredients:

All-purpose flour (maida) - 2 cups

Ghee or melted butter - 3 tbsp

Salt - 1/2 tsp

Cottage cheese (paneer), crumbled - 1 cup

Corn kernels, boiled - 1/2 cup

Onion, finely chopped - 1 small

Ginger, minced - 1 inch piece

Green chili, chopped - 1

Cumin seeds - 1/2 tsp

Red chili powder - 1/4 tsp

Coriander powder - 1/2 tsp

Lemon juice - 1 tbsp

Coriander leaves, finely chopped - a handful

Oil for frying and sautéing

Cooking Directions:

Alright, first things first, we've got to set the stage, and that means prepping our dough. Flour, salt, and a generous dose of ghee come together in an embrace. Mix them, knead them with water, let them get to know each other until they're a soft, cooperative dough. Give it a rest for 30 minutes; every artist needs their downtime.

Now, the spotlight's on our main act. Heat up some oil in a pan and throw in the cumin seeds. Let them pop and sizzle, setting the rhythm. In goes the onion, ginger, and green chili, laying down the backing tracks.

Here comes the melody: crumbled cottage cheese and boiled corn. Let them jive and mingle. Red chili powder, coriander powder, they're our background vocalists, adding depth and character. As things heat up, toss in the fresh coriander leaves. And to wrap it all up? A zesty note of lemon juice.

Back to our patient dough. Roll it, shape it, and then, the grand finale: filling it with our star duo. Seal them up and they're ready for their stage dive into a pot of hot oil, emerging golden and crispy.

Behold, the Cottage Cheese & Corn Samosas. Crispy on the outside, a harmonious duet of flavors on the inside. Perfect to enjoy while listening to some smooth jazz, or you know, just a quiet evening at home. Cheers to good food and great tunes!

Enjoy

9. Butternut Squash Samosas

Alright, folks, imagine autumn in a bite. The falling leaves, the comforting embrace of a sweater, and the warmth of a fireplace. Butternut squash epitomizes that essence and today, we're taking it on a slightly exotic journey. Prepare to be transported!

Prep: 30 min. Cook: 40 min. Ready in: 1 h. 10 min. Servings: 4

Ingredients:

All-purpose flour (maida) - 2 cups

Ghee or melted butter - 3 tbsp

Salt - 1/2 tsp

Butternut squash, peeled and diced - 2 cups

Onion, finely chopped - 1 medium

Garlic, minced - 3 cloves

Cumin seeds - 1/2 tsp

Red chili flakes - 1/4 tsp

Ground nutmeg - a pinch

Ground cinnamon - a pinch

Brown sugar - 1 tbsp

Lemon juice - 1 tsp

Fresh coriander leaves, finely chopped - a handful

Oil for frying and sautéing

Cooking Directions:

Here we go. We start with our trusty base – the dough. Flour, a sprinkle of salt, and our ghee. Mix, knead, add water, and make that beautiful, soft dough. Let it nap for a bit; about 30 minutes should do.

Now, the heart of this story – our butternut squash. In a pan, splash in some oil, sizzle the cumin seeds till they're fragrant, and throw in those onions and garlic. Saute them till they're soft and golden, but let's not rush. Good things take time, remember?

In goes our butternut squash, dancing around like those autumn leaves in the wind. Now, the spices, just hints to keep things intriguing: red chili flakes for warmth, a pinch of nutmeg and cinnamon to remind you of holiday pies, and a spoon of brown sugar to sweeten the deal. Let it cook, stir, become one harmonious medley. And then, a splash of lemon juice for that touch of brightness, and fresh coriander for a zing.

Back to our rested dough. Roll it out, cut it, and then – the piece de resistance – fill it with our autumnal mix. Seal them tight, then deep-fry these beauties until they're golden and oh-so-tempting.

And there you have it, Butternut Squash Samosas, a culinary ode to autumn. Best enjoyed with a view of falling leaves, a good book, or just good company. Here's to the magic of seasons and flavors.

Enjoy

10. Potato and Feta Samosas

Picture this: the earthiness of sweet potatoes meeting the tangy saltiness of feta cheese. An unexpected duo, yet one that creates a mouth-watering symphony of flavors. It's a blend of rustic simplicity with a touch of Mediterranean flair. Ready for this adventure?

Prep: 25 min. Cook: 40 min. Ready in: 1 h. 5 min. Servings: 4

Ingredients:

All-purpose flour (maida) - 2 cups

Ghee or melted butter - 3 tbsp

Salt - 1/2 tsp

Sweet potatoes, peeled and diced - 2 cups

Feta cheese, crumbled - 3/4 cup

Red onion, finely chopped - 1 medium

Garlic, minced - 2 cloves

Ground cumin - 1/2 tsp

Ground coriander - 1/2 tsp

Paprika - 1/4 tsp

Fresh mint, chopped - a handful

Lemon zest - 1 tsp

Olive oil for sautéing

Oil for frying

Cooking Directions:

First up, let's create the canvas - our dough. Flour, ghee, salt - mix these together and knead, adding water slowly until you've got a soft, pliable dough. Set it aside, let it rest and dream of its soon-to-be filling for about 30 minutes.

Meanwhile, in a pan, warm up that olive oil. Toss in the red onions and garlic. Let them sweat, let them sing until they're soft and fragrant. Add in those sweet potatoes, our star of the evening. Saute them until they're soft and have a hint of caramelization.

Sprinkle in the ground cumin, coriander, and paprika. Stir, let the spices get friendly with those sweet potatoes. Once the sweet potatoes are cooked and mushy, crumble in that feta cheese. Add the fresh mint and lemon zest, and give it one final stir, ensuring that every bite is a flavor explosion.

Back to our waiting dough. Roll it out, create pockets and stuff them with this Mediterranean inspired filling. Seal the edges, then deep fry until they're golden, crisp, and whispering promises of deliciousness.

And voila! Sweet Potato & Feta Samosas on your plate. A culinary journey that took you from the homely fields to sun-kissed Mediterranean coasts. Dig in, enjoy the contrast, and let your palate explore. Until next time, eat well and travel through flavors.

Enjoy

11. Spicy Lamb Samosas

Stepping into the hustle and bustle of a Middle Eastern souk, the aroma of spices wafting through the air, and the distant sizzle of meat cooking. That's the ambiance we're diving into with these Spicy Lamb Samosas. Let the culinary journey commence.

Prep: 35 min. Cook: 45 min. Ready in: 1 h. 20 min. Servings: 4

Ingredients:

All-purpose flour (maida) - 2 cups

Ghee or melted butter - 3 tbsp

Salt - 1/2 tsp

Ground lamb - 500 grams

Onion, finely chopped - 1 large

Garlic, minced - 3 cloves

Ginger, grated - 1 inch

Green chili, finely chopped - 2

Ground turmeric - 1/4 tsp

Ground cumin - 1/2 tsp

Ground coriander - 1/2 tsp

Red chili powder - 1/4 tsp

Tomato, finely chopped - 1 large

Fresh cilantro, chopped - a handful

Mint leaves, chopped - a handful

Lemon juice - 1 tbsp

Oil for frying and sautéing

Cooking Directions:

First, we craft our envelope. Flour, a little salt, ghee – simple ingredients coming together. Add water, knead to a soft consistency, and let it rest while we tackle the vibrant filling.

In a heated pan, glug in some oil. Throw in the onions, garlic, ginger, and those fiery green chilies. Stir until the onions are translucent, and you're enveloped by an aromatic symphony. Now, let's introduce our hero – the ground lamb. Cook until browned, breaking it apart as you go.

Dust those spices – turmeric, cumin, coriander, and red chili powder. The kitchen's going to smell like that souk in no time. Now, a juicy tomato joins the party, and we let it cook until the lamb is well-coated and juicy. Finish with a sprinkle of cilantro, mint, and a squeeze of lemon.

Rolling back to our dough – make it thin, cut circles, fill them up with the spiced lamb magic, and seal them tight. Deep fry these packets until they're golden and irresistibly crisp.

Here we are. Spicy Lamb Samosas, a pocketful of Middle Eastern promise. Close your eyes, take a bite, and let the flavors transport you to bustling streets and vibrant markets. Until our next culinary escapade, stay curious and keep tasting.

Enjoy

12. Chicken Tikka Samosas

Ah, the beloved chicken tikka - India's global culinary ambassador. Today, it sneaks into a crispy pocket, reinventing itself in the form of a samosa. The journey from tandoor to deep-fryer is nothing short of legendary.

Prep: 30 min. Cook: 50 min. Ready in: 1 h. 20 min. Servings: 4

Ingredients:

All-purpose flour (maida) - 2 cups

Ghee or melted butter - 3 tbsp

Salt - 1/2 tsp

Chicken breast, diced - 500 grams

Plain yogurt - 4 tbsp

Red onion, finely chopped - 1

Garlic, minced - 3 cloves

Ginger, grated - 1 inch

Ground turmeric - 1/4 tsp

Red chili powder - 1/2 tsp

Garam masala - 1/2 tsp

Ground cumin - 1/2 tsp

Ground coriander - 1/2 tsp

Lemon juice - 2 tbsp

Fresh cilantro, chopped - a handful

Oil for frying and marinating

Cooking Directions:

Let's begin with the casing. Combine flour, ghee, and salt. Knead with water, making a soft dough. Let it take a short nap, resting for about 30 minutes.

While our dough dreams, we're off to craft a chicken tikka masterpiece. In a mixing bowl, tumble in the chicken dices, plain yogurt, ginger, garlic, lemon juice, and all our aromatic spices – turmeric, red chili, cumin, coriander, and the magical garam masala. Give it a good mix, ensuring each chicken piece is cloaked in this marinating magic. Let it sit, let the flavors meld for about 20 minutes.

Heat a skillet and pour in a touch of oil. Introduce your red onions, let them soften, then usher in your marinated chicken. Cook until the chicken's done, absorbing all those fabulous spices. Finish with a sprinkle of fresh cilantro.

Back to the dough, roll it out. Circles of potential ready to be filled with our tikka delight. Seal them with intent, then deep fry until they've achieved that perfect golden hue.

There you have it, Chicken Tikka Samosas – a fusion of flavors, a dance of traditions. Best enjoyed hot, let every bite take you on a journey through the bustling streets of Delhi or Mumbai. Here's to many more flavor adventures!

Enjoy

13. Beef Keema Samosas

Imagine the bustling bylanes of an Indian market, with keema stalls lined up, wafting out irresistible aromas. Now, put that robust, spicy keema into a flaky samosa, and you've got a culinary masterpiece right there. Intrigued? Let's jump right into it.

Prep: 30 min. Cook: 55 min. Ready in: 1 h. 25 min. Servings: 4

Ingredients:

All-purpose flour (maida) - 2 cups

Ghee or melted butter - 3 tbsp

Salt - 1/2 tsp

Ground beef - 500 grams

Green peas - 1 cup

Onion, finely chopped - 1 large

Garlic, minced - 3 cloves

Ginger, grated - 1 inch

Green chili, finely chopped - 2

Ground turmeric - 1/4 tsp

Ground cumin - 1/2 tsp

Ground coriander - 1/2 tsp

Garam masala - 1/2 tsp

Tomato puree - 4 tbsp

Fresh cilantro, chopped - a handful

Oil for frying and sautéing

Cooking Directions:

Begin with the base. Mix the flour, ghee, and salt. Knead with water till you get a pliable dough. Once done, let it rest and dream about the spicy filling it's about to embrace.

In the world of fillings, keema reigns supreme. Heat a dash of oil in a pan. Fry onions till they're golden, then add ginger, garlic, and those zesty green chilies. As they sizzle and sing, toss in the ground beef. Cook until it's brown and aromatic. Now, it's time for the spices - turmeric, cumin, coriander, and that aromatic garam masala. Stir well. Pour in the tomato puree, let it simmer, merging with the meat. Add in the green peas and cook until they're soft and the flavors are beautifully melded together. Sprinkle in some cilantro to wrap up the filling.

Roll out the dough, cut into circles, stuff with the keema magic, and seal them. Fry until they're golden and perfect.

Voila! Beef Keema Samosas are ready to be devoured. Crispy on the outside, flavorful on the inside, this is street food at its finest, ready for the taking. Dive in, savor, and reminisce about an Indian marketplace evening.

Enjoy

14. Turkey and Pea Samosas

If ever there was a time to reimagine the classic Thanksgiving turkey, it's now. Who needs an oven when you've got hot oil, and who needs a table when you've got your hands? Let's travel off the beaten path and make turkey the star of our samosa show.

Prep: 30 min. Cook: 50 min. Ready in: 1 h. 20 min. Servings: 4

Ingredients:

All-purpose flour (maida) - 2 cups

Ghee or melted butter - 3 tbsp

Salt - 1/2 tsp

Ground turkey - 500 grams

Green peas - 1 cup

Red onion, finely chopped - 1 large

Garlic, minced - 3 cloves

Ginger, grated - 1 inch piece

Green chili, finely chopped - 1

Ground turmeric - 1/4 tsp

Ground cumin - 1/2 tsp

Ground coriander - 1/2 tsp

Garam masala - 1/2 tsp

Fresh cilantro, chopped - a handful

Oil for frying and sautéing

Cooking Directions:

Alright, first things first. Let's tackle the shell. Mix together the flour, ghee, and a pinch of salt. Knead it, and add water little by little until you've got a soft dough. Cover it up and let it sit for a while.

Now, for the heart of our samosa – the filling. In a pan, get some oil shimmering. Toss in the onions and wait till they're dancing a golden jig. Add in the ginger, garlic, and the fiery green chili. Let them sizzle, releasing their fragrant aroma. Next up, the turkey. Cook until it's lost its pink and is basking in the spicy melody.

Time for the seasonings. In goes the turmeric, cumin, coriander, and of course, the star – garam masala. Mix it well, let the turkey soak up the flavors. Introduce the peas, let them mingle, and then, sprinkle in the cilantro to give it a fresh finish.

Roll your dough, cut it, and stuff with this turkey goodness. Seal it and then into the hot oil it goes, frying to crispy perfection.

And there you have it – Turkey & Pea Samosas, a delightful twist to the traditional roast. Every bite, a testament to how food can bridge cultures. It might not replace your Thanksgiving dinner, but it sure will earn a place at the table.

Enjoy

15. Chicken and Mushroom Samosas

Ever find yourself torn between the desire for an earthy, comforting mushroom soup and the crispy allure of a chicken samosa? Me too. So, let's resolve that inner culinary conflict by marrying the two in this Chicken & Mushroom Samosa.

Prep: 35 min. Cook: 50 min. Ready in: 1 h. 25 min. Servings: 4

Ingredients:

All-purpose flour (maida) - 2 cups

Ghee or melted butter - 3 tbsp

Salt - 1/2 tsp

Chicken breast, minced - 500 grams

White button mushrooms, chopped - 1 cup

Onion, finely diced - 1 medium

Garlic, minced - 3 cloves

Ginger, grated - 1-inch piece

Green chili, finely chopped - 1

Ground black pepper - 1/4 tsp

Ground cumin - 1/2 tsp

Soy sauce - 1 tbsp

Fresh thyme - 1 tsp

Oil for frying and sautéing

Cooking Directions:

Kick things off by prepping the dough. Flour, ghee, and a touch of salt — mix these bad boys together. Gradually add water, kneading until you've got a soft, cohesive dough. Tuck it under a cloth and let it dream of its crispy future.

Onto the main event, the filling. A dance of flavors and textures awaits. Heat some oil in your trusty pan, and in go the onions. Let them get all golden and aromatic. Now, the trifecta: ginger, garlic, and green chili. Stir it up until the fragrance takes over your kitchen. Slide in the minced chicken, cooking until it's no longer pink but golden.

As the chicken grooves, invite the mushrooms to the party. Let them cook down, releasing their earthy goodness. Spice it up with pepper, cumin, and then hit it with soy sauce for that umami depth. Finish with a sprinkle of fresh thyme.

Time to assemble. Roll out that rested dough, fill it with the chicken-mushroom wonder, and seal the treasure inside. Fry them up until they're audibly crispy and golden brown.

Here you have it, folks. Chicken & Mushroom Samosas - where East meets West, and rustic meets chic. Dive in and let every bite be a journey from a bustling Indian street to a cozy European café.

Enjoy

16. Lamb and Apricot Samosas

I often find myself captivated by the Silk Road's tales, that ancient trade route bridging East and West. And what better way to honor its legacy than with food? Introducing the Lamb & Apricot Samosas, a beautiful confluence of Middle Eastern flavors in the beloved Indian appetizer.

Prep: 40 min. Cook: 50 min. Ready in: 1 h. 30 min. Servings: 4

Ingredients:

All-purpose flour (maida) - 2 cups

Ghee or melted butter - 3 tbsp

Salt - 1/2 tsp

Ground lamb - 500 grams

Dried apricots, finely chopped - 1/2 cup

Onion, finely diced - 1 large

Garlic, minced - 4 cloves

Ginger, grated - 1-inch piece

Ground cumin - 1 tsp

Ground coriander - 1 tsp

Smoked paprika - 1/2 tsp

Fresh rosemary, chopped - 1 tsp

Fresh mint, chopped - a handful

Oil for frying and sautéing

Cooking Directions:

Alright, my friends, first things first. For our trusty vessel, the samosa shell, mix together the flour, ghee, and salt. Add water in increments, kneading as you go, until you've got a supple dough. Let it rest, dream, and relax under a moist cloth.

For our filling, a tale of rich and sweet. Warm up that pan, drizzle in some oil, and toss the onions until they whisper tales of caramelization. The fragrance trio - ginger, garlic, and a hint of cumin - joins in next. Once those fragrances mingle and rise, slide in the ground lamb, browning it to perfection.

Now, for the star-crossed lovers: apricots and spices. Toss them into the pan, letting the apricots' sweetness embrace the lamb's richness. A dash of paprika, a sprinkle of coriander, rosemary, and our dish begins to take shape. As a finishing touch, fresh mint joins the party.

Once you've got that flavorful mash, roll out your dough into circles, stuff them with the lamb mixture, and seal their fate. Fry these beauties until they've achieved that delectable golden hue.

And there you are! Lamb & Apricot Samosas. A bite that's a journey, from the bustling bazaars of Delhi to the fragrant souks of Marrakech. Paired with a minty dip or a cool raita, it's an experience not to be missed. Eat, savor, and let the stories flow.

Enjoy

17. Duck and Hoisin Sauce Samosas

Picture this: Beijing's sprawling streets, a lively night market, and the intoxicating aroma of Peking duck wafting through. Now, let's recreate that memory but with an Indian twist. I present to you the Duck & Hoisin Sauce Samosas.

Prep: 45 min. Cook: 50 min. Ready in: 1 h. 35 min. Servings: 4

Ingredients:

All-purpose flour (maida) - 2 cups

Ghee or melted butter - 3 tbsp

Salt - 1/2 tsp

Duck breast, finely chopped - 500 grams

Hoisin sauce - 4 tbsp

Green onions, chopped - 1/2 cup

Ginger, minced - 1-inch piece

Garlic, minced - 3 cloves

Sesame oil - 1 tbsp

Soy sauce - 2 tbsp

Fresh cilantro, chopped - 2 tbsp

Red chili flakes - 1/2 tsp

Oil for frying and sautéing

Cooking Directions:

First off, the vessel. For that iconic samosa crust, mix together your flour, ghee, and a pinch of salt. Gradually add water, kneading until it's soft and pliable. Let it take a little nap under a damp cloth.

Onto our filling, where East truly meets East. Begin with your pan. A dash of sesame oil heats up, and in go the green onions, ginger, and garlic. The sizzle, the aroma - oh, it's like music! Into this aromatic base, introduce the finely chopped duck. Cook it until it's browned and almost crispy.

Now, for that sweet and salty symphony: a generous drizzle of hoisin sauce, a splash of soy, and a sprinkle of chili flakes. Mix it all together, let the flavors meld and finish with a handful of fresh cilantros.

Roll out the dough into circles, ladle in that delectable duck filling, and seal them tight. Into hot oil they go, frying to perfection.

Sink your teeth into one of these, and it's a ticket straight to those Beijing streets, with a pit stop in Mumbai. These Duck & Hoisin Sauce Samosas - where tradition meets innovation, and every bite is a delightful surprise. Pair it with a cold beer or a glass of wine, and you're set for the evening. Cheers to culinary adventures!

Enjoy

18. Chicken and Spinach Samosas

Picture a bistro in the heart of Provence. A plate of tender chicken sautéed with fresh greens. Now, translate that to a bustling Indian street. That's where the Chicken & Spinach Samosas come into play - a seamless blend of universal comfort and the vibrancy of Indian spices

Prep: 40 min. Cook: 50 min. Ready in: 1 h. 30 min. Servings: 4

Ingredients:

All-purpose flour (maida) - 2 cups

Ghee or melted butter - 3 tbsp

Salt - 1/2 tsp

Chicken breast, finely chopped - 500 grams

Fresh spinach, chopped - 2 cups

Onion, finely diced - 1 large

Garlic, minced - 4 cloves

Ginger, grated - 1-inch piece

Ground turmeric - 1/2 tsp

Ground cumin - 1 tsp

Ground coriander - 1 tsp

Chili powder - 1/2 tsp

Lemon juice - 2 tbsp

Oil for frying and sautéing

Cooking Directions:

Let's dive in, shall we? Start with the dough, a combination of flour, ghee, and salt. Knead with care, gradually adding water until you get a soft, welcoming dough. Cover it with a damp cloth, and let it daydream for a bit.

Next, the heart of our samosa. Warm up a skillet, splash in some oil, and get those onions going until they're golden. Then the aromatic duo: ginger and garlic. Toss in the chicken and let it cook until it's no longer pink but beautifully golden. Spices come in next - turmeric, cumin, coriander, and a touch of chili. Let them all get to know each other.

Spinach's the last main act. It might seem like a lot, but trust me, it'll wilt down to perfection. A splash of lemon juice for that tang, and you're good to go.

Now, to assemble. Roll out your dough, fill it with this lush chicken-spinach mix, and seal them tight. Deep-fry them until they wear a crispy, golden coat.

Here you have it - a little bit of France, a lot of India, all tucked into a crispy package. Chicken & Spinach Samosas: the world on a plate, one bite at a time. Pair them with a refreshing mint chutney and embark on a global journey from the comfort of your dining room. Bon Appétit or as we say in India, Khaan paan ka aanand lo!

Enjoy

19. Pork and Apple Samosas

Imagine an autumn day in New England. Apple orchards stretching out as far as the eye can see, and there's a slight chill in the air. Pigs roasting over an open fire. Now, bring that imagery to the bustling streets of New Delhi. That's our Pork & Apple Samosas: a harmonious blend of sweet and savory, of East and West.

Prep: 40 min. Cook: 45 min. Ready in: 1 h. 25 min. Servings: 4

Ingredients:

All-purpose flour (maida) - 2 cups

Ghee or melted butter - 3 tbsp

Salt - 1/2 tsp

Pork shoulder, finely chopped - 500 grams

Green apples, finely diced - 2

Brown sugar - 2 tbsp

Cinnamon - 1 tsp

Ground clove - 1/4 tsp

Nutmeg - a pinch

Fresh thyme - 1 tsp

Garlic, minced - 3 cloves

Onion, finely chopped - 1

Salt and pepper to taste

Oil for frying and sautéing

Cooking Directions:

Alright, first things first. Let's get the soul of the samosa ready. Mix the flour, ghee, and salt together. Gradually add in water and knead, like you're giving it a gentle massage, until you get a soft, welcoming dough. Let it sit, covered with a damp cloth, letting those flavors marinate.

Onto the star of the show - the filling. Start with a good ol' pan, heat some oil, and toss in those onions. You want them just on the brink of caramelization. Slide in the garlic and let it work its aromatic magic. Now, in goes the pork, cooking it until it's browned and glorious.

The apple comes next. Toss it in, followed by brown sugar, and those warming spices - cinnamon, clove, nutmeg. It's like a comforting hug on a cold day. Season with salt, pepper, and fresh thyme, then stir until everything's melded beautifully.

For the assembly: roll out the dough, spoon in that rich pork-apple mixture, and seal these pockets of delight. Fry them till they're golden and crisp, ready to surprise anyone with the burst of flavors within.

And there you have it, folks - the magic of fall wrapped up in an Indian package. Pork & Apple Samosas: where orchards meet spice markets. Perfect with a side of spiced cranberry chutney and a glass of bourbon. Close your eyes, take a bite, and let the flavors waltz across your palate

Enjoy

20. Chicken Curry Samosas

Sometimes, all you need is a classic, a recipe that takes you back to the heart of where it all began. Enter the Chicken Curry Samosas – an ode to the quintessential Indian curry, with all its spices and richness, wrapped in a crisp package.

Prep: 45 min. Cook: 50 min. Ready in: 1 h. 35 min. Servings: 4

Ingredients:

All-purpose flour (maida) - 2 cups

Ghee or melted butter - 3 tbsp

Salt - 1/2 tsp

Chicken breast, finely chopped - 500 grams

Onions, finely sliced - 2

Tomatoes, finely chopped - 2

Ginger-garlic paste - 2 tbsp

Red chili powder - 1 tsp

Ground turmeric - 1/2 tsp

Garam masala - 1 tsp

Ground coriander - 1 tsp

Ground cumin - 1/2 tsp

Fresh cilantro, chopped - a handful

Yogurt - 2 tbsp

Salt to taste

Oil for frying and sautéing

Cooking Directions:

First, the base. That's our dough. Flour, salt, and ghee come together in a passionate dance, with water playing the tune. The result is a smooth and soft dough. Let it rest, like a rockstar before the big gig.

The filling, ah, that's where the fun begins. Heat some oil, throw in the onions, and cook until they're golden-brown, dripping with stories of Indian kitchens. Ginger-garlic paste jumps in next, sizzling and telling tales of old recipes. In go the chicken pieces, dancing and turning golden. Tomatoes follow, breaking down, lending their tanginess to the mix.

Spices! Red chili, turmeric, coriander, cumin, and the king of them all - garam masala. Stir it up, let them mingle, create the magic. A dollop of yogurt to mellow it down, simmer until it's all rich and glorious. Finish with fresh cilantro because what's curry without that green freshness?

Assembling time: roll out the dough, fill in with the curry, seal them up tight. And into the hot oil they go, until they wear that perfectly golden hue.

There you go, a journey through India, one bite at a time. Chicken Curry Samosas, where tradition meets innovation, where home meets adventure. Best served with tamarind chutney and a side of nostalgia.

Enjoy

21. Tuna and Potato Samosas

Picture this: The Mediterranean meets the bustling streets of Mumbai. A beautiful marriage of the deep blue sea and the vibrant spices of the subcontinent. That's the essence of our Tuna & Potato Samosas. A dish where Europe shakes hands with Asia.

Prep: 40 min. Cook: 45 min. Ready in: 1 h. 25 min. Servings: 4

Ingredients:

All-purpose flour (maida) - 2 cups

Ghee or melted butter - 3 tbsp

Salt - 1/2 tsp

Canned tuna, drained and flaked - 300 grams

Potatoes, boiled and mashed - 3 medium-sized

Green chilies, finely chopped - 2

Fresh lemon juice - 1 tbsp

Coriander powder - 1 tsp

Ground cumin - 1/2 tsp

Fresh cilantro, chopped - a handful

Salt and pepper to taste

Oil for frying and sautéing

Cooking Directions:

Kick things off with the dough. Mix that flour, ghee, and a pinch of salt. Gradually welcome water into the mix, kneading until you've got a smooth, supple dough. Let it sit quietly, contemplating its destiny.

Now, the heart of the matter: the filling. Warm up some oil in a pan. Sprinkle in the cumin seeds, letting them pop and sizzle, waking up all those dormant flavors. In goes the green chili for that spicy kick and the tuna, letting it soak in all those flavors. The mashed potatoes join the party next, binding it all together. Season with salt, pepper, coriander powder, and a generous squeeze of fresh lemon juice. Mix it all together, and just before you're done, sprinkle in that fresh cilantro. It's like the confetti at the end of a great party.

The assembly line's next. Roll out the dough, spoon in that hearty filling, and fold them up, sealing all that goodness inside. Dive them into hot oil until they're golden and irresistibly crunchy.

So here they are, the globetrotters. Tuna & Potato Samosas, a journey from the coasts of Spain to the spice markets of India. Grab a cold beer, maybe a slice of lemon, and let's toast to the beautiful fusion of flavors and cultures.

Enjoy

22. Shrimp and Cilantro Samosas

Ah, the ocean's jewels - shrimp. Combine that with the earthy, pungent aroma of cilantro and you're setting sail on an epicurean voyage. Dive into the Shrimp & Cilantro Samosas, where waves of flavor crash against the shores of tradition.

Prep: 50 min. Cook: 45 min. Ready in: 1 h. 35 min. Servings: 4

Ingredients:

All-purpose flour (maida) - 2 cups

Ghee or melted butter - 3 tbsp

Salt - 1/2 tsp

Fresh shrimp, peeled and finely chopped - 300 grams

Garlic, minced - 3 cloves

Green chilies, finely chopped - 2

Ground cumin - 1 tsp

Fresh cilantro, chopped - a big handful

Lemon zest - from 1 lemon

Salt and pepper to taste

Oil for frying and sautéing

Cooking Directions:

First things first. Our dough. Mix the flour, ghee, and salt in a harmonious blend. As you introduce water, knead with love and care, crafting a dough as smooth as the ocean on a calm day. Give it time, let it rest.

Now, onto the soul of this dish - the filling. Heat a splash of oil in a pan. A hint of garlic, the warmth of green chilies, and then, the star of the show - the shrimp. Toss them around until they're pink and proud. Now, sprinkle that cumin, a touch of salt, and a generous pinch of pepper. As the aromas start weaving tales of seaside towns, throw in a shower of fresh cilantro and a zest of lemon, a bright burst of citrus. Crafting time. Stretch out that dough, fill it with tales of the sea, and fold. Crisp them up in golden baths of hot oil.

And there you have it. A masterpiece. Shrimp & Cilantro Samosas, where the heart of the sea meets the soul of the land. Crack one open, hear the crunch, taste the sea, and let the flavors dance on your palate. Here's to memories, adventures, and a plateful of joy.

Enjoy

23. Salmon and Dill Samosas

Ah, the cold waters of the Northern seas. A place where salmon glide gracefully, bearing the tales of deep fjords and vast oceans. Now, imagine that salmon dancing with fragrant dill, encased in a crisp shell. Welcome to the Salmon & Dill Samosas saga.

Prep: 45 min. Cook: 40 min. Ready in: 1 h. 25 min. Servings: 4

Ingredients:

All-purpose flour (maida) - 2 cups

Ghee or melted butter - 3 tbsp

Salt - 1/2 tsp

Fresh salmon, finely chopped - 300 grams

Fresh dill, chopped - a hearty bunch

Onions, finely chopped - 1 medium

Lemon juice - 2 tbsp

Ground black pepper - 1/2 tsp

Capers, roughly chopped - 1 tbsp

Salt to taste

Oil for frying and sautéing

Cooking Directions:

Begin by romancing the dough. Mingle the flour, ghee, and salt. Gradually whisper in some water, kneading into a poised, elegant dough. Let it rest; it's preparing for the dance ahead.

For the main act, the filling: Drizzle oil in a pan. Welcome the onions, letting them turn translucent, sharing stories of their layers. Introduce the salmon; watch them flirt and turn a blushing pink. Time for the dill to waltz in, with capers making their quirky entrance. Season it - salt, pepper, and the lemon's bright notes.

As the narrative unfolds, roll out that dough. Place the filling, a blend of sea and herb, and seal them up. Deep fry until they wear a golden, radiant gown.

Feast your eyes on these beauties! The Salmon & Dill Samosas, where Scandinavia meets the heart of Delhi. Bite into a symphony of flavors, and as the flaky salmon and aromatic dill dance on your tongue, raise a toast to the harmony of worlds coming together.

Enjoy

24. Crab and Cream Cheese Samosas

You ever dance with a crab on a starlit beach? No? Well, imagine the richness of crab meat waltzing with creamy cheese inside a pocket that's crispier than a moonlit night. That's our story tonight with Crab & Cream Cheese Samosas.

Prep: 50 min. Cook: 40 min. Ready in: 1 h. 30 min. Servings: 4

Ingredients:

All-purpose flour (maida) - 2 cups

Ghee or melted butter - 3 tbsp

Salt - 1/2 tsp

Lump crab meat - 300 grams

Cream cheese, softened - 200 grams

Green onions, finely chopped - 3 stalks

Worcestershire sauce - 1 tsp

Ground white pepper - 1/4 tsp

Salt to taste

Oil for frying and sautéing

Cooking Directions:

Start with the canvas - the dough. Blend together the flour, ghee, and a hint of salt. Sing a lullaby as you add water, kneading until it's as smooth as jazz on a summer's eve. Let it nap.

For the heart of our tale - the filling: In a bowl, marry the lump crab meat and cream cheese. They're the Romeo and Juliet of our culinary saga. Slide in the green onions for a touch of freshness, a splash of Worcestershire for depth, and season with salt and that refined white pepper.

When the story elements are set, roll out our dough into sheets thinner than a lover's whisper. Spoon our creamy-crab love story in the center, fold and seal their destiny. Gently lay them in hot oil, frying until they wear a golden hue.

Voilà! The stars of our evening - Crab & Cream Cheese Samosas. A rendezvous of ocean depth with creamy dreams. Pop one in, and let the creamy crabby magic whisk you to coastal serenades. Here's to stories, flavors, and moonlit dances

Enjoy

25. Lobster and Saffron Samosas

Imagine diving deep into the azure Mediterranean, finding treasures of opulent lobster, then soaring high above to the saffron fields of Spain. This evening, we're bringing that riveting adventure to your plate with Lobster & Saffron Samosas.

Prep: 55 min. Cook: 40 min. Ready in: 1 h. 35 min. Servings: 4

Ingredients:

All-purpose flour (maida) - 2 cups

Ghee or melted butter - 3 tbsp

Salt - 1/2 tsp

Lobster meat, cooked and chopped - 300 grams

Saffron strands - a generous pinch

Warm milk - 2 tbsp

Garlic, minced - 3 cloves

Flat leaf parsley, chopped - 2 tbsp

Lemon zest - 1 tsp

Ground black pepper - 1/2 tsp

Salt to taste

Oil for frying and sautéing

Cooking Directions:

Embark on this journey with the dough. In a bowl, rally the flour, ghee, and salt. As you sprinkle water, knead with the passion of a flamenco dancer until it's smooth and ready to rest.

For the grand spectacle - the filling: Steep the saffron in warm milk; let it paint the milk gold. In a pan, kiss it with some oil, and serenade the garlic until it's aromatic. Enter the lobster, the king of our tale. Drizzle the golden saffron milk, and let them revel in this golden bath. Jazz it up with parsley, lemon zest, and the seasonings.

With the stage set, roll out the dough into thin sheets. Bestow upon them the lobster-saffron blend, fold, and seal their fates. Fry in hot oil until they're as golden as a Mediterranean sunset.

And there you have it! Lobster & Saffron Samosas, a dish where oceans meet golden fields. Each bite, an embrace of luxury and history. Enjoy this with a fine wine or a song in your heart, and let the flavors dance on your palate.

Enjoy

26. Sardine and Tomato Samosas

Close your eyes and think of a rustic coastal village, where the scent of fresh sardines grilling over an open flame mingles with the laughter of locals. Tonight, we're bringing that seaside charm to your plate with Sardine & Tomato Samosas.

Prep: 45 min. Cook: 35 min. Ready in: 1 h. 20 min. Servings: 4

Ingredients:

All-purpose flour (maida) - 2 cups

Ghee or melted butter - 3 tbsp

Salt - 1/2 tsp

Sardines, deboned and flaked - 200 grams

Tomatoes, deseeded and finely chopped - 2 large

Red onion, finely chopped - 1 medium

Capers, finely chopped - 2 tbsp

Fresh basil, chopped - a handful

Olive oil - 1 tbsp

Lemon juice - 1 tsp

Ground black pepper - 1/2 tsp

Salt to taste

Oil for frying

Cooking Directions:

Begin the gig with the dough. In a spacious bowl, let the flour, salt, and that glorious ghee meet. Work them into a soft dough, adding water as you go. Once it's all harmonious, cover it up and let it rest for about 30 minutes.

Onto our dynamic duo. In a pan, heat some oil and toss in the cumin seeds. Wait for them to perform their opening act, then usher in the onions, garlic, ginger, and green chili. Let them groove together until the onions are golden.

Now, in with the lentils. These legumes have soaked, boiled, and are ready to party. Add them to the pan, followed by the finely chopped spinach. Shower the mix with coriander powder and garam masala. Let them mingle, groove, and become one. Once everything's nice and cooked, a splash of lemon juice to lift the mood.

Now, our rested dough is back in the limelight. Roll it out, slice it into the desired shape, and fill each with our lentil-spinach melody. Seal them up and get them ready for their final act.

Into the oil they go, frying until they're a perfect golden brown, crispy on the outside, soulful on the inside.

Et voilà! Sardine & Tomato Samosas. A perfect ode to those little coastal towns where life's simple, and flavors are profound. Dive into this oceanic delight with a chilled beer in hand and let the waves of flavor wash over you.

Enjoy

27. Mackerel and Onion Samosas

Imagine wandering through the bustling streets of Kerala, where the air is thick with the scent of frying fish, tempered spices, and the distant lure of the Arabian Sea. Today, we're on a journey to this spice haven with Mackerel & Onion Samosas.

Prep: 40 min. Cook: 35 min. Ready in: 1 h. 15 min. Servings: 4

Ingredients:

All-purpose flour (maida) - 2 cups

Ghee or melted butter - 3 tbsp

Salt - 1/2 tsp

Mackerel, deboned and flaked - 250 grams

Onions, thinly sliced - 2 medium

Green chilies, finely chopped - 2

Ginger-garlic paste - 1 tsp

Mustard seeds - 1/2 tsp

Curry leaves - a sprig

Ground turmeric - 1/4 tsp

Oil for frying and sautéing

Salt to taste

Cooking Directions:

Begin with the canvas - the dough. The holy trinity of flour, ghee, and salt awaits in a bowl. Pour in water and knead, invoking the spirit of the monsoons until it's soft and supple. As it rests, we head to the heart of our Kerala escapade.

Now, for the heart and soul of our tale: the filling. Let your pan sing with hot oil, pop in the mustard seeds, and let them crackle like firecrackers on Diwali night. The ginger-garlic paste and green chilies enter the fray, followed closely by the sliced onions. As they start to caramelize, with stories of the coast whispered between them, bring in the mackerel. Season, add the turmeric, and watch as it all transforms into a golden, fragrant delight.

With your dough ready for action, roll out discs and fill them with our spicy mackerel mixture. Fold, seal, and drop them into hot oil. Fry until they're as golden as a Malabar coast sunset.

Feast your senses on these Mackerel & Onion Samosas. It's more than a bite; it's a passage through time and space to the coastlines of southern India. Best enjoyed with coconut chutney and dreams of the sea.

Enjoy

28. Calamari and Lemon Samosas

The Mediterranean calls! Think sun-kissed shores, a glass of ouzo, and the tang of citrus in the air. That's right! Tonight, we're jetting off to Greece in spirit, with these Calamari & Lemon Samosas.

Prep: 50 min. Cook: 30 min. Ready in: 1 h. 20 min. Servings: 4

Ingredients:

All-purpose flour (maida) - 2 cups

Ghee or melted butter - 3 tbsp

Salt - 1/2 tsp

Calamari rings, thinly sliced - 250 grams

Lemon zest - 1 tbsp

Lemon juice - 1 tbsp

Fresh parsley, finely chopped - a handful

Garlic cloves, minced - 2

Red chili flakes - 1/2 tsp

Olive oil - 2 tbsp

Salt and black pepper to taste

Oil for frying

Cooking Directions:

Alright, first things first. Let's lay down the groundwork. In your trusty mixing bowl, summon the flour, ghee, and salt. Slowly add water, kneading until you've got a dough that's smoother than a Greek god's pick-up line. Let it rest, dreaming of Athenian adventures.

Now, let's get to the star of this Grecian saga: the filling. Heat olive oil like the midday Mediterranean sun. Gracefully introduce the minced garlic, letting it dance till it's just golden. Toss in those calamari rings – they'll sizzle, they'll pop, they're ready to rock. Season with salt, pepper, and a hint of chili flakes. Now, for the pièce de résistance, sprinkle the lemon zest, drizzle the juice, and fold in that fresh parsley. Mix it all up, and let those flavors do the Sirtaki.

With our dough now wide awake, roll it out into flat rounds. Spoon in our calamari concoction. Fold. Seal. Dive them into hot oil until they're as golden as a Santorini sunset.

There you have it! Calamari & Lemon Samosas. One bite, and you're on a balcony overlooking the Aegean, with bouzouki music playing in the distance. So, pour yourself a glass of white, and let the Mediterranean dreams flow.

Enjoy

29. Anchovy and Capers Samosas

Ah, the Amalfi Coast – where azure seas meet ancient cliffs. Here's a recipe that will sail you straight to Italy, with flavors so vivid, you can almost feel the sea breeze. Let's embark on a culinary journey with Anchovy & Capers Samosas.

Prep: 40 min. Cook: 30 min. Ready in: 1 h. 10 min. Servings: 4

Ingredients:

All-purpose flour (maida) - 2 cups

Ghee or melted butter - 3 tbsp

Salt - 1/2 tsp

Anchovy fillets, finely chopped - 100 grams

Capers, roughly chopped - 3 tbsp

Red onion, finely diced - 1 medium

Tomato, deseeded and finely chopped - 1 medium

Olive oil - 2 tbsp

Black olives, pitted and chopped - 2 tbsp

Fresh parsley, finely chopped - 2 tbsp

Salt and black pepper to taste, but be cautious with salt due to the anchovies

Oil for frying

Cooking Directions:

Start with the foundation. In your trusted bowl, combine flour, ghee, and that pinch of salt. Slowly introduce water, and knead till you get a dough that's reminiscent of the rolling Italian countryside. Let it relax; perhaps imagine it sunbathing in Positano.

Now, onto our star-studded filling. Warm the olive oil in a pan, singing an old Neapolitan tune. Add in the red onion, sautéing until it whispers tales of Vesuvius. Toss in the anchovies, letting them melt into the mix, followed by the tomatoes, capers, and olives. Stir it up, feeling the rhythm of a tarantella. Finish off with fresh parsley and season, though easy on the salt – remember, those anchovies have tales of the salty sea to tell.

Our well-rested dough is now ready for its moment in the spotlight. Roll it out, fill with our coastal concoction, fold, and seal. Fry them up till they're golden, reminiscent of a sun setting on the Tyrrhenian Sea.

And voilà! Anchovy & Capers Samosas, a bite that will transport you straight to a seaside trattoria, with waves crashing and mandolins strumming. Pop open a bottle of Chianti, and let the Mediterranean dream take over.

Enjoy

30. Prawn Masala Samosas

Imagine the bustling streets of Mumbai – tuk-tuks, vibrant colors, the aroma of spices filling the air. Now, let's embark on a journey to the heart of India, with flavors so bold, they narrate stories of centuries-old traditions. Presenting, the Prawn Masala Samosas.

Prep: 45 min. Cook: 30 min. Ready in: 1 h. 15 min. Servings: 4

Ingredients:

All-purpose flour (maida) - 2 cups

Ghee or melted butter - 3 tbsp

Salt - 1/2 tsp

Prawns, shelled and deveined - 200 grams

Onion, finely chopped - 1 medium

Tomato puree - 3 tbsp

Ginger-garlic paste - 1 tsp

Turmeric powder - 1/4 tsp

Red chili powder - 1/2 tsp

Garam masala - 1/2 tsp

Cumin seeds - 1/2 tsp

Coriander leaves, finely chopped - a handful

Salt to taste

Oil for frying

Cooking Directions:

First, we lay our groundwork. In your favorite bowl, bring together flour, ghee, and salt. Gradually add water, kneading it until it's as smooth as a Bollywood ballad. Let it sit; perhaps dreaming of star-studded film premieres.

Now, let's stir up the drama with our filling. In a pan, heated to perfection, pop in the cumin seeds. As they sizzle and dance, introduce the onions. Sauté them till they're golden, just like a Bollywood heroine's outfit. Slide in the ginger-garlic paste, letting it serenade the onions. Now, the prawns make their grand entrance, getting cozy with the spices. Drizzle in the tomato puree, and season with turmeric, red chili powder, and garam masala. The prawns cook swiftly, absorbing all those incredible flavors. End the act with freshly chopped coriander.

Roll out your dough, dreaming of cinematic love stories. Fill it with the prawn masala saga, fold, and seal them up. Deep fry till they're a perfect golden hue, mirroring the awards of Bollywood.

And there you have it, Prawn Masala Samosas. One bite, and you're amidst the magic of Mumbai's movie sets, with rhythmic dance numbers and melodious tunes. Pour yourself a masala chai, and let the Bollywood dream take center stage.

Enjoy

31. Mozzarella and Tomato Samosas

Ah, bella Italia! Land of Renaissance art, ancient ruins, and... samosas? That's right, I'm taking you on a detour to the romantic streets of Rome, with a twist that Leonardo da Vinci would've appreciated. Let's dive into the Mozzarella & Tomato Samosas.

Prep: 40 min. Cook: 25 min. Ready in: 1 h. 5 min. Servings: 4

Ingredients:

All-purpose flour (maida) - 2 cups

Ghee or melted butter - 3 tbsp

Salt - 1/2 tsp

Mozzarella cheese, cubed - 200 grams

Tomatoes, deseeded and finely chopped - 2 medium

Basil leaves, finely chopped - a handful

Olive oil - 2 tbsp

Garlic, minced - 2 cloves

Balsamic vinegar - 1 tsp

Black pepper to taste

Oil for frying

Cooking Directions:

Firstly, we craft our canvas. In a trusty bowl, bring together the flour, ghee, and salt. Gently pour in water, kneading with the passion of an Italian opera until smooth. Let it rest; maybe it's dreaming of gondola rides in Venice.

For our main act, the filling: In a sizzling pan, pour in that golden olive oil, add the seductive garlic, letting it whisper sweet nothings to the oil. Gently introduce the tomatoes, allowing them to soak up all the flavors. Now, with the pan off the heat, welcome the mozzarella and fresh basil, drizzling in that balsamic vinegar for an extra kick. Season with love, and a dash of black pepper.

Now, paint with your dough. Roll it out, fill it with the heart of Italy, fold, and seal them with a kiss. Fry until they're golden and crispy, reminiscent of a Tuscan sunset.

There you have it, Mozzarella & Tomato Samosas, a culinary masterpiece. One bite and you're serenaded by Andrea Bocelli, amidst the rolling hills and picturesque vineyards. Pour a glass of Chianti, close your eyes, and 'Viva l'Italia!'.

Enjoy

32. Blue Cheese and Walnut Samosas

Alright, my friends, hold onto your berets. We're taking a detour to the quaint bistros of Paris. The elegance of blue cheese, the crunch of walnuts, all inside the golden embrace of a samosa. Intrigued? Let's embark on this Blue Cheese & Walnut Samosa adventure.

Prep: 40 min. Cook: 25 min. Ready in: 1 h. 5 min. Servings: 4

Ingredients:

All-purpose flour (maida) - 2 cups

Ghee or melted butter - 3 tbsp

Salt - 1/2 tsp

Blue cheese, crumbled - 150 grams

Walnuts, toasted and chopped - 100 grams

Honey - 2 tbsp

Fresh rosemary, finely chopped - 1 tsp

Black pepper to taste

Oil for frying

Cooking Directions:

Let's start by building the foundation. In your trusty bowl, mix the flour, ghee, and salt. Gradually add water, kneading it till it's as harmonious as a French chanson. Let it take a little nap; it's probably daydreaming about the Seine River.

Now, onto our pièce de résistance, the filling. In a mixing bowl, bring together the crumbled blue cheese and toasted walnuts. Drizzle in the honey, just enough for a hint of sweetness. Sprinkle in the fresh rosemary and season with freshly ground black pepper. Give it a gentle mix, let those flavors dance a passionate tango.

Roll out that rested dough, thinking of all the art and history of Montmartre. Fill it with that Parisian concoction, fold, and seal those treasures inside. Deep fry till they take on a shade reminiscent of the golden lights on the Eiffel Tower at night.

And voilà, Blue Cheese & Walnut Samosas. Each bite, a love letter to the City of Light. Serve with a glass of Bordeaux and let the flavors transport you to a jazz-filled evening by the Champs-Élysées.

Enjoy

33. Brie and Cranberry Samosas

We're sticking around France for this one, but I've got a twist. The creaminess of Brie, the tang of cranberries, wrapped in a crispy shell. A rendezvous of sophistication and playfulness. Let's get started on these Brie & Cranberry Samosas, shall we?

Prep: 40 min. Cook: 25 min. Ready in: 1 h. 5 min. Servings: 4

Ingredients:

All-purpose flour (maida) - 2 cups

Ghee or melted butter - 3 tbsp

Salt - 1/2 tsp

Brie cheese, cubed - 200 grams

Dried cranberries - 100 grams

Fresh thyme leaves - 1 tsp

Zest of 1 lemon

Black pepper to taste

Oil for frying

Cooking Directions:

First things first, the dough. In your mixing bowl, whisk together the flour, ghee, and a touch of salt. Add water incrementally, kneading until the dough is as smooth as a ballroom dance at Versailles. Let it rest a bit, dreaming of the French countryside.

Now, for our pièce de théâtre - the filling. Gently toss together the Brie cubes and dried cranberries in a bowl. Sprinkle in the fresh thyme leaves, and zest that lemon like it owes you money. Season with black pepper for a bit of bite.

Next, awaken your dough and roll it out, reminiscing about a picnic near the Loire Valley. Cradle your filling in the center, fold over, and seal like a secret love letter. Now, let them dance in hot oil until they're golden and tempting.

Mes amis, feast your eyes (and soon, your taste buds) on these Brie & Cranberry Samosas. Paired with a crisp white wine, they're the stuff dreams are made of. Here's to enjoying the finer things in life, from our own kitchens.

Enjoy

34. Cheddar and Onion Samosas

Alright, time to put on some Beatles because we're taking a quick hop across the Channel to England. Picture this: classic British cheddar meets fragrant onions, spiced just right, all bundled up in our trusted samosa blanket. Ready for this Anglo-Indian masterpiece? Let's make some Cheddar & Onion Samosas.

Prep: 35 min. Cook: 25 min. Ready in: 1 h. Servings: 4

Ingredients:

All-purpose flour (maida) - 2 cups

Ghee or melted butter - 3 tbsp

Salt - 1/2 tsp

Sharp cheddar cheese, grated - 200 grams

Onions, finely chopped - 2 medium-sized

Green chilies, finely chopped - 2 (optional)

Fresh cilantro, chopped - a handful

Ground cumin - 1/2 tsp

Oil for frying

Cooking Directions:

Kick things off with the dough. Flour, ghee, and salt come together in your mixing bowl. Add water bit by bit, kneading until you have a dough that's as firm and steadfast as the British monarchy. Give it a little rest; it's probably daydreaming of double-decker buses.

While the dough's chilling, let's whip up that filling. In a pan with a touch of oil, sauté your onions until they're translucent and singing Elton John hits. Throw in the green chilies if you're feeling adventurous. Then, off the heat, mix in that lovely cheddar, fresh cilantro, and sprinkle with cumin for a hint of warmth.

Roll out your dough, thinking of misty mornings in the English countryside. Stuff with that cheesy-oniony goodness, fold, and seal these little packets of joy. Fry them up until they're as golden as the last rays of an English summer sunset.

And there you have it! Cheddar & Onion Samosas, a match made in Anglo-Indian heaven. Pair with a stout or, dare I say, a cuppa tea, and let your taste buds set sail on the Thames.

Enjoy

35. Gouda and Spinach Samosas

Hop on, we're taking a culinary ride to the Netherlands. Canals, windmills, tulips... and cheese. Glorious Gouda, to be precise. Combine that with the lush green of spinach and we're in for a treat. Roll up your sleeves and let's whip up some Gouda & Spinach Samosas, a nod to Amsterdam's finest.

Prep: 40 min. Cook: 25 min. Ready in: 1 h. 5 min. Servings: 4

Ingredients:

All-purpose flour (maida) - 2 cups

Ghee or melted butter - 3 tbsp

Salt - 1/2 tsp

Gouda cheese, grated - 200 grams

Fresh spinach, chopped - 200 grams

Garlic, minced - 3 cloves

Nutmeg, grated - a pinch

Red chili flakes - 1/2 tsp (optional)

Salt & pepper to taste

Oil for frying

Cooking Directions:

First order of business: the dough. In that trusty mixing bowl of yours, combine the flour, ghee, and salt. Gently add water, kneading into a firm, cooperative dough. Once it's come together, let it take a little nap, probably dreaming of cycling beside tulip fields.

While that's resting, let's tackle the filling. Over medium heat, sauté your garlic until it's fragrant. Toss in the spinach and cook until wilted and rich. Now, gently mix in that creamy Gouda, the nutmeg, and some chili flakes if you like a kick. Season to perfection with salt and pepper. When you're rolling out your dough, think of Dutch artistry - from Van Gogh's swirls to Vermeer's precision. Place your delightful filling in the middle, fold them up, and seal them like cherished secrets. Into the hot oil they go, until they're beautifully golden and irresistible.

Voila! Gouda & Spinach Samosas, a piece of Amsterdam in every bite. Perfect with a cold beer or a glass of crisp white wine. Enjoy and let the flavors transport you to the vibrant streets of the Dutch capital.

Enjoy

36. Ricotta and Herb Samosas

Close your eyes. Imagine the serenity of the Italian countryside. Vineyards, olive groves, and a gentle breeze that carries the melody of an Italian love song. Now imagine the delicate flavors of ricotta and fresh herbs dancing on your tongue. That's what we're making today. Let's create some edible poetry with these Ricotta & Herb Samosas.

Prep: 35 min. Cook: 25 min. Ready in: 1 h. Servings: 4

Ingredients:

All-purpose flour (maida) - 2 cups

Ghee or melted butter - 3 tbsp

Salt - 1/2 tsp

Ricotta cheese - 200 grams

Mixed fresh herbs (basil, parsley, chives), finely chopped - 1/2 cup

Lemon zest - 1 tsp

Garlic, minced - 2 cloves

Salt & pepper to taste

Red chili flakes - 1/4 tsp (optional)

Oil for frying

Cooking Directions:

First thing's first, let's get that dough rolling. Into your bowl goes the flour, ghee, and salt. As you gently add water and knead, think of Italian grandmothers making pasta by hand, pouring love into every move. Once you've got a firm dough, let it rest. It's probably serenading the sunset.

For the filling, it's all about simplicity and fresh flavors. In a bowl, mix that creamy ricotta with the herbs, garlic, and lemon zest. Add a touch of chili flakes if you like, and season with the spirit of Italy: salt and a generous twist of black pepper.

Now, channel your inner Michelangelo as you roll out your dough, stuff it with the ricotta mixture, and sculpt these little masterpieces. Seal them up and deep-fry until they're golden and singing 'Volare'.

Here they are, Ricotta & Herb Samosas, little pockets of Italian joy. Pair with a glass of Prosecco and toast to la dolce vita. Buon appetito and let the romance of Italy sweep you away.

Enjoy

37. Feta and Olive Samosas

Ah, the Mediterranean! Sandy beaches, cerulean waters, and flavors that resonate with soulful melodies. The salty charm of feta, paired with olives, is reminiscent of a Greek taverna overlooking the Aegean Sea. Today, we're blending the crunch of India with the heart of Greece in these Feta & Olive Samosas.

Prep: 40 min. Cook: 25 min. Ready in: 1 h. 5 min. Servings: 4

Ingredients:

All-purpose flour (maida) - 2 cups

Ghee or melted butter - 3 tbsp

Salt - 1/2 tsp

Feta cheese, crumbled - 200 grams

Black and green olives, chopped - 1/2 cup

Tomatoes, finely chopped and drained - 1/2 cup

Red onion, finely diced - 1/4 cup

Fresh oregano, chopped - 1 tbsp

Lemon zest - 1 tsp

Salt & pepper to taste

Oil for frying

Cooking Directions:

Alright, my friend, dough first. In your trusty bowl, unite the flour, ghee, and salt. As you pour in water and knead, let your mind wander to sun-kissed Greek islands. Once you have a firm dough, give it some downtime to soak in the Mediterranean sun.

On to the filling. Imagine the bustle of a Greek market. In a bowl, toss together the crumbled feta, olives, tomatoes, red onion, and oregano. The lemon zest? That's the sunny Greek sky. If you're feeling adventurous, throw in a pinch of salt and pepper.

Now, let's roll. Channel the rhythm of a Greek dance as you roll out your dough, fill them with our Mediterranean mixture, and fold them into perfect pockets of flavor. A quick swim in hot oil, and they're sunbathing to a golden perfection.

There you have it, Feta & Olive Samosas, a taste of Greece in every bite. Pour yourself a glass of ouzo or a crisp white wine, maybe toss in some sirtaki music, and transport yourself to a breezy evening on Mykonos. Opa!

Enjoy

38. Camembert and Fig Samosas

Ah, France. Rolling vineyards, countryside chateaus, and a love affair with cheese that's simply poetic. When you think of Camembert, perhaps you imagine a rustic French picnic with a backdrop of lavender fields. Today, we're taking that romance and giving it an Indian twist. Say 'bonjour' to the decadent Camembert & Fig Samosas.

Prep: 40 min. Cook: 25 min. Ready in: 1 h. 5 min. Servings: 4

Ingredients:

All-purpose flour (maida) - 2 cups

Ghee or melted butter - 3 tbsp

Salt - 1/2 tsp

Camembert cheese, cubed - 200 grams

Figs, finely chopped - 1/2 cup

Honey - 2 tbsp

Walnuts, toasted and chopped - 1/4 cup

Fresh thyme leaves - 1 tsp

Black pepper - 1/4 tsp

Oil for frying

Cooking Directions:

Let's start with our base. The dough. In your go-to mixing bowl, whisk together the flour, ghee, and salt. Slowly add water, imagining the gentle flow of the Seine through Paris, and knead till it's as smooth as Edith Piaf's voice. Give it a breather; let it daydream about Montmartre.

Now, for the pièce de résistance – the filling. In a cozy bowl, you're going to mix the soft Camembert cubes with the sweet figs. Drizzle in the honey, like sunlight through French shutters. Toss in your toasted walnuts, thyme leaves, and a crackling of black pepper.

Time to play! Roll out the dough, hum a little La Vie En Rose, and spoon in that gorgeous French melody of a filling. Fold them into beautiful parcels and fry until they're as golden as the fields of Provence.

Voilà! Camembert & Fig Samosas, straight from the heart of France, with a detour through Delhi. Pour some Bordeaux, set the table with your finest china, and travel with every bite from the bustling streets of Mumbai to a quiet café in Paris. Santé!

Enjoy

39. Mascarpone and Berry Samosas

The beauty of Italy and its desserts! Picture the narrow streets of Florence, gelato stands on every corner, and the sweet tunes of Puccini in the air. Now, we're taking that Italian sweet flair and encapsulating it in the golden crunch of a samosa. Ladies and gentlemen, prepare for the symphony that is Mascarpone & Berry Samosas.

Prep: 45 min. Cook: 25 min. Ready in: 1 h. 10 min. Servings: 4

Ingredients:

All-purpose flour (maida) - 2 cups

Ghee or melted butter - 3 tbsp

Salt - 1/2 tsp

Mascarpone cheese - 200 grams

Mixed berries (blueberries, raspberries, strawberries) - 1 cup

Powdered sugar - 1/4 cup, plus extra for dusting

Lemon zest - 1 tsp

Vanilla extract - 1 tsp

Mint leaves, finely chopped - a few

Oil for frying

Cooking Directions:

Let's dive into the dough. In your favorite mixing bowl – come on, everyone's got one – bring together the flour, ghee, and a pinch of salt. As you drizzle in water and knead, allow yourself to drift to a Venetian gondola ride, the sunset reflecting off the canals. Let your dough rest and dream of the Italian Riviera.

For the filling, ah, it's an aria of flavors. In another bowl, you'll whisk that creamy mascarpone with powdered sugar until smooth and velvety. Gently fold in those gorgeous, colorful berries. Their juicy pop of flavor, the tang, the sweetness, it's a dance of summer in Tuscany. Drizzle in vanilla and sprinkle that fragrant lemon zest. The mint? That's your encore.

Next, channel your inner artisan. Roll out that dough with passion, place that decadent filling in, and seal them with amore. Into the hot oil they go, where they'll transform into golden nuggets of joy.

And there you have it, my friend, a bite of Italy, wrapped in the soul of India. Dust them with powdered sugar, making it snow like a winter in Milan. Grab an espresso, or better yet, a limoncello, and toast to a journey that took you from the Indian subcontinent to the heart of Italy, all in one bite. Cin cin!

Enjoy

40. Swiss Cheese and Ham Samosas

Ah, the snow-capped peaks of the Swiss Alps! An inspiration for poets, artists, and... well, cheese lovers. Imagine the cool breeze, the distant sound of yodeling, and now, let's whisk that alpine fantasy into the lively streets of Mumbai. What do you get? Swiss Cheese & Ham Samosas.

Prep: 40 min. Cook: 20 min. Ready in: 1 h. Servings: 4

Ingredients:

All-purpose flour (maida) - 2 cups

Ghee or melted butter - 3 tbsp

Salt - 1/2 tsp

Swiss cheese, grated - 200 grams

Ham, finely diced - 150 grams

Spring onions, finely chopped - 2

Black pepper, freshly ground - 1/2 tsp

Mustard sauce - 1 tbsp

Chives, finely chopped - 2 tbsp

Oil for frying

Cooking Directions:

First, we craft the foundation. In that trusted mixing bowl of yours, the flour, ghee, and salt are going to become best pals. A little cold water, some vigorous kneading, and let this friendship solidify while it rests. Think of it as them sharing skiing tales by a warm fire.

While they reminisce, it's showtime for the cheese and ham. That beautifully melted Swiss cheese, the smoky bits of ham, and the fresh spring onions come together like a Swiss folk band. Throw in a grinding of black pepper, a dollop of mustard for that zing, and those chives, just to green it up. You're basically creating a mountain meadow in a bowl.

Onto the fun part. Roll out the dough and envision yourself setting up camp by Lake Geneva. Plop that filling in, wrap it up, and slide these beauties into hot oil, where they sizzle, bubble, and turn into crispy pockets of delight.

And voila! A blend of the Alpine charm and Indian zest. Serve them up hot with a cold pint or perhaps a crisp white wine, and let your taste buds ski down the slopes of flavor. Here's to the high life, both on the mountain and on your plate.

Enjoy

41. Egg and Sausage Samosas

Alright, folks, gather 'round. Remember those lazy Sunday brunches, the wafting scent of sizzling sausages, and eggs softly scrambling in a pan? We're taking those cherished brunch memories, rolling them up with some Indian magic, and boom! Egg & Sausage Samosas.

Prep: 30 min. Cook: 25 min. Ready in: 55 min. Servings: 4

Ingredients:

All-purpose flour (maida) - 2 cups

Ghee or melted butter - 3 tbsp

Salt - 1/2 tsp

Sausage, crumbled and cooked - 200 grams

Eggs, beaten - 4

Cheddar cheese, grated - 100 grams

Bell peppers, finely diced - 1/2 cup

Salt and pepper to taste

Chili flakes (optional) - 1/2 tsp

Oil for frying

Cooking Directions:

Start with the soul of any samosa, the dough. Combine that flour, ghee, and a sprinkle of salt. As it comes together with some cold water, you're not just making dough, you're crafting memories. Let it take a short nap while you prepare for the next step.

Over to the skillet. Crumble those sausages and let them sizzle away until they're golden brown. Time for the eggs to make an entrance. As they gently scramble, shower them with love, and by love, I mean cheddar cheese and bell peppers. Season it well, and maybe, just maybe, a hint of chili flakes for those who like to live on the wild side. Now, roll out that rested dough, dreaming of those Sunday mornings, and heap on that glorious filling. Seal them tight; these flavors shouldn't escape, not one bit. Fry these wonders till they're gorgeously golden.

There you have it! A bite of nostalgia, a taste of home, and a whirlwind tour of India, all in one samosa. Best paired with hot chai or a Bloody Mary if you're feeling particularly brunch-y. Here's to mornings that taste as good as they feel.

<u>Enjoy</u>

42. Bacon and Potato Samosas

Close your eyes. Imagine waking up in a log cabin, surrounded by pine trees, with the irresistible aroma of bacon wafting in. Now imagine that bacon, combined with the heartiness of potatoes, and tucked inside a samosa. Welcome to the Bacon & Potato Samosa experience.

Prep: 45 min. Cook: 25 min. Ready in: 1 h. 10 min. Servings: 4

Ingredients:

All-purpose flour (maida) - 2 cups

Ghee or melted butter - 3 tbsp

Salt - 1/2 tsp

Bacon, crisped and crumbled - 150 grams

Potatoes, boiled and mashed - 2 medium-sized

Green peas, boiled - 1/2 cup

Red onion, finely chopped - 1

Garlic cloves, minced - 2

Fresh rosemary, finely chopped - 1 tbsp

Salt and pepper to taste

Oil for frying

Cooking Directions:

Like any epic tale, we begin with the basics. In a bowl, the maida, ghee, and salt come together like old friends around a campfire. Add a touch of cold water, knead into a soft dough, and let it rest. Let it dream of tall trees and mountain breezes.

Now, for the soul of this samosa. In your favorite skillet, let the onions and garlic have a chat until translucent. Add those lovely mashed potatoes, green peas, and let them all get acquainted. Sprinkle in the fresh rosemary, salt, and pepper. The pièce de résistance? Crumbled, crispy bacon. Stir it all up and let the aroma envelop you.

The dough's rested enough. Roll it out, think of a morning sunrise, and spoon in that delightful filling. Seal them up, they're ready for their hot oil bath. Fry until they achieve that golden perfection.

And there you have it. Every bite is a journey through a rustic morning in the woods, the warmth of a log cabin, and the comfort of home. Pair it with a stout coffee or a spiced apple cider. To adventures, big and small, and to mornings that inspire.

Enjoy

43. Spinach and Feta Omelette Samosas

Picture this: a sunlit Greek morning, Mediterranean breezes carrying the scent of fresh herbs, and a palate tingling with the flavors of a fresh omelette – spinach and feta, to be precise. Now, let's infuse that Mediterranean moment with an Indian soul and pack it into a samosa.

Prep: 40 min. Cook: 25 min. Ready in: 1 h. 5 min. Servings: 4

Ingredients:

All-purpose flour (maida) - 2 cups

Ghee or melted butter - 3 tbsp

Salt - 1/2 tsp

Spinach, finely chopped - 2 cups

Feta cheese, crumbled - 150 grams

Eggs, whisked - 4

White onion, finely chopped - 1

Garlic cloves, minced - 2

Chili flakes - 1/2 tsp

Salt and pepper to taste

Oil for frying

Cooking Directions:

Let's kick things off with our dough. In a mixing bowl, whisk together maida, ghee, and a dash of salt. Now, gently add cold water, a little at a time, and knead into a firm, smooth dough. Once you've got that right, set it aside.

As for our star stuffing, get a pan hot and splash in some oil. In go the onions and garlic, sizzling and turning a lovely golden hue. Next, introduce the spinach, allowing it to wilt gracefully. Time to pour in the eggs, gently stirring until they're softly scrambled and just setting. Top it off with chili flakes, a seasoning of salt, pepper, and, last but definitely not least, our crumbled feta. Mix it up, then set aside to cool. Back to our dough. Roll it out into even circles and divvy up that glorious filling among them. Fold, pinch, seal, and they're ready for their golden makeover. Into the fryer they go until crispy perfection.

Here you are, a taste of Greece wrapped in an Indian embrace. Dip it into some tzatziki or mint chutney and take a bite. Here's to mornings that transport you, one flavor at a time.

Enjoy

44. Caramelized Onion and Goat Cheese Samosas

Imagine a French bistro tucked away in a Parisian alley, the air fragrant with the sweet allure of caramelizing onions. Now, whisk that aromatic dream into the heart of India with a crunchy samosa embrace. You ready? Let's embark on this journey.

Prep: 30 min. Cook: 35 min. Ready in: 1 h. 5 min. Servings: 4

Ingredients:

All-purpose flour (maida) - 2 cups

Ghee or melted butter - 3 tbsp

Salt - 1/2 tsp

Onions, thinly sliced - 3 large

Goat cheese, crumbled - 150 grams

Thyme, fresh or dried - 1 tsp

Brown sugar - 1 tbsp

Olive oil - 2 tbsp

Black pepper to taste

Oil for frying

Cooking Directions:

Firstly, for our sturdy vessel—the dough. Combine the maida, ghee, and a pinch of salt in a bowl. Slowly introduce cold water, mixing it in until you have a firm yet pliable dough. Give it a bit of a knead, then let it rest.

While that's taking a breather, heat the olive oil in a pan. Add the thinly sliced onions and let them sizzle, dance, and slowly transform into golden, caramelized goodness. Be patient—it's an art.

Halfway through, sprinkle in the brown sugar to enhance that caramel hue. Once the onions have achieved their rich, brown color and are beautifully softened, stir in the thyme and season with black pepper. Let it cool a bit before gently folding in the crumbled goat cheese. Now, back to our rested dough. Roll it into circles, place a generous helping of that onion and cheese mixture in the center, fold, and seal. Deep-fry these pockets of joy until they're golden and irresistible.

Pair with a glass of white wine or even a hot espresso, and let this Franco-Indian delight sweep you off your feet. Bon Appétit and Namaste!

Enjoy

45. Baked Beans and Cheese Samosas

You ever wake up with the sun shining through your window, the birds chirping, and think 'What I really want is a breakfast samosa?' No? Just me? Well, whether it's a regular craving or a new experiment, these baked beans and cheese samosas are the breakfast twist you never knew you needed.

Prep: 35 min. Cook: 20 min. Ready in: 55 min. Servings: 4

Ingredients:

All-purpose flour (maida) - 2 cups

Ghee or melted butter - 3 tbsp

Salt - 1/2 tsp

Canned baked beans - 1 cup

Cheddar cheese, grated - 1 cup

Red bell pepper, diced - 1

Jalapeño, finely chopped - 1

Cumin powder - 1/2 tsp

Oil - for frying

Cooking Directions:

Alright, let's dive in. Start with a large mixing bowl and get your flour in there. Mix in the ghee or melted butter and salt. Add just enough water to form a smooth yet firm dough. Cover it up with a damp cloth and give it a rest for about 20 minutes.

While that's setting, let's handle our filling. In a medium bowl, mix the canned baked beans, grated cheddar cheese, diced bell pepper, chopped jalapeño, and a sprinkle of cumin powder. Give it a good mix until you think everything's gotten to know each other.

Time to work that dough. Divide it into small balls and roll them out into circles, about 6 inches in diameter. Slice that circle in half. Now, you have two semi-circles, and each one is about to become the golden pocket that holds our delicious filling.

With the straight edge of the semi-circle towards you, place a hefty spoonful of your filling on one side. Then, fold the other side over it and press the edges to seal. Use a fork to crimp those edges and ensure that none of that cheesy, beany goodness tries to escape.

Now, heat your oil in a deep frying pan over medium heat. Once it's hot, but not smoking, slide in your samosas. Fry them until they're golden and crispy, which should be about 3 to 4 minutes on each side. Use a slotted spoon to remove and drain on paper towels.

There you have it — a breakfast spin on the classic samosa. These golden pockets of joy might not replace your morning coffee, but they'll surely make a delightful partner to it. Enjoy, and here's to trying new things at breakfast!

Enjoy

46. Avocado and Egg Samosas

So, here's a twist. A classic breakfast item meets an Indian street food favorite. If avocado toast and traditional samosas had a baby, this would be their delicious offspring. Let's embark on this culinary adventure.

Prep: 25 min. Cook: 20 min. Ready in: 45 min. Servings: 4

Ingredients:

All-purpose flour (maida) - 2 cups

Ghee or melted butter - 3 tbsp

Salt - 1/2 tsp

Avocado, ripe and mashed - 1

Eggs, boiled and chopped - 4

Red onion, finely diced - 1/2

Green chilies, finely chopped - 2

Lemon juice - 2 tsp

Fresh cilantro, chopped - a handful

Salt and pepper - to taste

Oil - for frying

Cooking Directions:

First up, the dough. In your trusty mixing bowl, toss in the flour, then mix in the ghee or melted butter and salt. Gradually add water until you've got a smooth but firm dough. Once you've achieved that perfection, cover it with a damp cloth and set it aside for a short nap of about 20 minutes.

While our dough dreams of becoming crispy samosas, let's get that filling ready. In a separate bowl, toss in the mashed avocado, boiled and chopped eggs, diced red onion, chopped green chilies, lemon juice, and fresh cilantro. Mix it all up and season with salt and pepper.

Now back to our well-rested dough. Divide it into small balls and roll each one into a circle, roughly 6 inches across. Cut that circle in half, creating two eager semi-circles. On one side of each semi-circle, spoon in your avocado and egg mixture. Fold the other side over the filling and press down on the edges. Crimp with a fork to make sure everything stays inside.

Heat your oil in a deep pan over medium heat. Wait for it to get just the right amount of hot, and carefully slide in the samosas. Fry them until they reach that mouth-watering golden color, about 3-4 minutes on each side. Lift them out with a slotted spoon and let them rest on paper towels.

And just like that, you've journeyed from the classic streets of Delhi to a hipster café in Brooklyn and back. These samosas are perfect for brunch, a snack, or honestly, any meal of the day. Dig in, enjoy, and always remember - breakfast doesn't have to be boring.

Enjoy

47. Ham and Pineapple Samosas

You ever find yourself stuck between the joy of a tropical vacation and the comfort of a hometown diner? These samosas are the embodiment of that delightful dilemma. Ham and pineapple, a controversial pizza topping, but an unapologetically tasty samosa filling.

Prep: 25 min. Cook: 20 min. Ready in: 45 min. Servings: 4

Ingredients:

All-purpose flour (maida) - 2 cups

Ghee or melted butter - 3 tbsp

Salt - 1/2 tsp

Ham, diced - 1 cup

Pineapple, diced into small pieces - 1 cup

Mozzarella cheese, shredded - 1/2 cup

Green bell pepper, finely diced - 1/2

Red chili flakes - 1 tsp

Salt and pepper - to taste

Oil - for frying

Cooking Directions:

Let's make the magic happen. Starting with the dough, in a mixing bowl, combine the flour, ghee or melted butter, and salt. Gradually pour in water, kneading until you're left with a smooth, firm dough. Once it's ready, cover it up with a damp cloth and let it rest for about 20 minutes.

In the meantime, let's talk filling. In another bowl, toss together the diced ham, pineapple bits, shredded mozzarella, finely diced bell pepper, and red chili flakes. Give it a good mix, then season with salt and pepper to your heart's content.

Now, back to our patiently waiting dough. Divide it into small balls and roll each one into a 6-inch circle. Slice each circle in half, and you've got yourself a pair of semi-circles. Place a spoonful of that irresistible ham and pineapple mixture on one side of each semi-circle. Fold the other side over, pressing down the edges, and crimping with a fork to seal all that goodness in.

In a deep pan, heat up your oil over medium heat. When it's shimmering and ready, slide in the samosas. Fry these bad boys until they turn a golden shade of delicious, about 3-4 minutes per side. Once cooked, use a slotted spoon to scoop them out, letting them drain on paper towels.

Who would've thought? A touch of tropical in a crispy Indian classic. Forget pizza debates; this is the new controversial duo in town. And trust me, once you've had a bite, you'll be firmly in the 'pro' camp.

Enjoy

48. Nutella and Banana Samosas

So, we're diving into the realm of desserts, and what's more indulgent than the sinful combination of Nutella and bananas? They say breakfast is the most important meal of the day, but I say, why not have a breakfast-flavored dessert?

Prep: 20 min. Cook: 15 min. Ready in: 35 min. Servings: 4

Ingredients:

All-purpose flour (maida) - 2 cups

Ghee or melted butter - 3 tbsp

Salt - a pinch

Nutella - 1 cup

Banana, sliced into small pieces - 2

Cinnamon powder - 1/2 tsp

Powdered sugar - for dusting (optional)

Oil - for frying

Cooking Directions:

First and foremost, let's tackle that dough. Take a bowl, and into it goes the flour, ghee or melted butter, and that tiny pinch of salt. Gradually add water, mixing and kneading until the dough is firm and smooth. Cover the bowl with a damp cloth and let our dough have a short 20-minute nap.

While it's resting, let's create some magic with the filling. In another bowl, merge the Nutella and banana slices. Add a sprinkle of cinnamon powder and give it a gentle stir.

It's showtime for our dough. Split it into small balls and roll each one out into about a 6-inch circle. Divide each circle into two, making semi-circles. With utmost care, place a dollop of the Nutella-banana mix on one side of the semi-circle. Bring the other half over to meet it, and press the edges to seal the deal. Crimp them with a fork, ensuring no tasty escapees.

Heat oil in a deep pan over a medium flame. Once it's shimmering and ready to roll, in go the samosas. Fry them to perfection, which is a crispy, golden brown - about 3 minutes on each side should do the trick. Use a slotted spoon to fish them out and let them rest on paper towels to drain.

Dust with some powdered sugar if you're feeling extra fancy. Dive into this delectable treat where the lushness of Nutella meets the freshness of bananas, all wrapped up in a crispy shell. This, my friends, is where breakfast meets dessert in a love story for the ages.

Enjoy

49. Peanut Butter and Jelly Samosas

Ah, the PB&J, a true staple of lunchboxes from coast to coast. Today, we're giving this childhood favorite a cosmopolitan makeover, presenting it in a form you've never experienced before. You think you know the peanut butter & jelly sandwich? Well, brace yourself.

Prep: 20 min. Cook: 15 min. Ready in: 35 min. Servings: 4

Ingredients:

All-purpose flour (maida) - 2 cups

Ghee or melted butter - 3 tbsp

Salt - a pinch

Creamy peanut butter - 1 cup

Jam of your choice (strawberry, raspberry, etc.) - 1 cup

Chopped roasted peanuts - 1/4 cup (optional)

Oil - for frying

Cooking Directions:

Start off with the base – the dough. Into your mixing bowl, add the flour, ghee or melted butter, and that pinch of salt. Slowly introduce water, mixing and kneading your way to a firm yet pliable dough. Once achieved, drape it with a damp cloth and let it rest for about 20 minutes.

During that downtime, let's jazz up the filling. In a bowl, mix together the creamy peanut butter and jam. For a little surprise crunch, fold in the chopped roasted peanuts.

Now, back to our rested dough. Split it into evenly sized balls and roll each one into a circle, about 6 inches in diameter. Slice each circle into two, forming semi-circles. Spoon a generous helping of the PB&J mix onto one half of each semi-circle. Gently fold over the other half, sealing the edges to trap that gooey goodness inside. For extra security, crimp the edges with a fork.

Now for the golden transformation. Heat oil in a pan on medium. Once you see those first tiny bubbles, slide in the samosas. Fry until they achieve that glorious golden brown hue – roughly 3 minutes on each side. Scoop them out with a slotted spoon and let them sit on paper towels, shedding any excess oil.

Serve these bad boys while they're hot and watch as a simple lunchtime sandwich transcends into an evening gourmet experience. PB&J might've been child's play once, but now? It's all grown up.

Enjoy

50. Granola and Yogurt Samosas

Morning rituals often involve bowls of granola and dollops of yogurt. But, my friend, mornings can sometimes feel boring, and that's where we spice things up a bit. Let's bring the breakfast spirit to our samosas.

Prep: 25 min. Cook: 15 min. Ready in: 40 min. Servings: 4

Ingredients:

All-purpose flour (maida) - 2 cups

Ghee or melted butter - 3 tbsp

Salt - a pinch

Plain yogurt - 1 cup

Granola mix - 1 cup (preferably with nuts and dried fruits)

Honey - 2 tbsp (or more as per taste)

Oil - for frying

Cooking Directions:

Begin with the backbone of our creation – the dough. Toss that flour into a big bowl, throw in the ghee or melted butter, and sprinkle in that pinch of salt. Begin to mix, and slowly add water. Your target is a firm dough that's just begging to be kneaded. Once you've got that consistency, cover it with a damp cloth and let it sit and contemplate life for about 20 minutes.

While our dough is in deep thought, we'll make the filling. In a separate bowl, blend the yogurt, granola, and honey. Mix until you have a harmonious union of creaminess and crunch.

Back to our dough. Once it's done pondering the meaning of existence, divide it into even balls and roll each one into a 6-inch circle. Halve each circle to get semi-circles. Onto one half of each semi-circle, spoon your granola-yogurt blend. Lift the other half over and pinch those edges tight. Use a fork for a fancy crimped look.

Time to introduce our samosas to the pan. Heat your oil on medium until it's bubbling with excitement. Gently slide in the samosas. They should take about 3 minutes on each side to achieve a sun-kissed golden tan. Once they're looking fabulous, get them out with a slotted spoon and let them relax on paper towels to shake off any extra oil.

Dive in while they're hot. Morning, noon, or night, these samosas are the embodiment of breakfast freedom. Enjoy every crunchy, creamy bite. You've just transformed your morning routine.

Enjoy

51. Apple Pie Samosas

Apple pie: an American classic. Samosas: a beloved Indian snack. It's a cultural mishmash, a testament to how diverse flavors can come together to create something mind-blowing. Let's make some culinary magic.

Prep: 30 min. Cook: 20 min. Ready in: 50 min. Servings: 4

Ingredients:

All-purpose flour (maida) - 2 cups

Ghee or melted butter - 3 tbsp

Salt - a pinch

Apples - 2 large, peeled, cored, and finely chopped

Brown sugar - 1/2 cup

Cinnamon - 1 tsp

Nutmeg - 1/4 tsp

Lemon juice - 1 tbsp

Oil - for frying

Cooking Directions:

Let's get started with our trusty dough. In a spacious bowl, mix the flour, ghee or melted butter, and a pinch of salt. Slowly add water and start the magical process of kneading. Aim for a firm yet pliable dough. Once achieved, let it take a short nap under a damp cloth for about 20 minutes.

For the filling, your apples will play the leading role. Take those finely chopped apples and toss them in a pan over medium heat. As they start to sizzle and soften, rain down the brown sugar, sprinkle in the cinnamon and nutmeg, and squeeze in that zesty lemon juice. Stir occasionally, and let this sweet symphony cook until the apples are soft and the mixture thickens. Then, let it cool down. No one likes a steamy filling.

Back to our well-rested dough. Split it into even balls and roll each out into a 6-inch circle. Divide each circle into halves. On one end of the semi-circle, you're going to spoon in your apple filling. Lift the other half over the top and seal those edges. For an added touch of class, crimp with a fork.

Your frying pan is the stage for the final act. Heat up that oil on a medium flame. When it's good and ready, introduce the samosas. Give them about 3 minutes each side to reach the pinnacle of crispy golden perfection. When they're just right, rescue them with a slotted spoon and let them cool their heels on some paper towels.

Now, take a moment. Bite in. Close your eyes. It's apple pie, it's a samosa, it's everything right with fusion food. Grab a scoop of vanilla ice cream if you're feeling particularly adventurous.

Enjoy

52. Chocolate and Marshmallow Samosas

Picture this: the crisp of a samosa paired with the nostalgia of campfire s'mores. This one's an unusual creation, born from my insatiable sweet tooth and love for fusion foods. It might raise some eyebrows in traditional samosa-making circles, but trust me on this one.

Prep: 30 min. Cook: 20 min. Ready in: 50 min. Servings: 4

Ingredients:

For the dough:

1 cup all-purpose flour

2 tablespoons oil or ghee

A pinch of salt

Water, as needed

For the filling:

1 cup semisweet chocolate chips

1 cup mini marshmallows

1 tablespoon unsweetened cocoa powder

2 tablespoons heavy cream

1 teaspoon vanilla extract

A pinch of salt

To finish:

Oil, for frying

Powdered sugar, for dusting (optional)

Cooking Directions:

Let's dive into this, shall we?

First, we're making our canvas - the dough. In a mixing bowl, combine the flour, salt, and oil. Gradually add water, mixing it in until you get a firm yet pliable dough. Knead it for a good 5 minutes; give it some love, it deserves it. Once it's smooth, cover it with a damp cloth and let it rest for about 20 minutes.

While our dough is taking a nap, let's work on the filling. In a saucepan over medium heat, melt the chocolate chips, cocoa powder, heavy cream, and vanilla extract. Stir it together until silky smooth, and then take it off the heat.

When you're ready to assemble, divide your dough into small balls. Roll each one out into a flat circle, and then cut it in half. On one side of your semi-circle, spoon some marshmallows and drizzle over the chocolate mixture.

Now, for the fun part. Fold the dough over, pressing the edges to seal. Remember, no one likes a leaky samosa, especially when it's filled with liquid gold like this.

Heat oil in a deep frying pan. Once it's hot but not smoking, in go the samosas. Fry them until they're a beautiful golden-brown color on both sides. Once done, place them on paper towels to drain the excess oil.

Sprinkle with powdered sugar if you're feeling extra indulgent. You now have a dessert that bridges the gap between East and West, tradition and innovation. Enjoy these while warm, and watch as the chocolate and marshmallow meld in a delightful dance of flavors.

Enjoy

53. Mango and Coconut Samosas

Okay, gather 'round, adventurers. We're about to embark on a tropical journey that takes the best of two worlds and mashes them up into a palm-sized package of delight. It's where the exotic sweetness of mangoes meets the creamy richness of coconut.

Prep: 35 min. Cook: 20 min. Ready in: 55 min. Servings: 4

Ingredients:

For the dough:

1 cup all-purpose flour

2 tablespoons oil or ghee

A pinch of salt

Water, as needed

For the filling:

1 cup ripe mango, finely chopped

½ cup desiccated coconut

2 tablespoons condensed milk

1 teaspoon lime zest

A pinch of cardamom powder

To finish:

Oil, for frying

Toasted coconut flakes, for garnish

Cooking Directions:

Let's make some magic.

Kick things off with our trusty dough. In your trusty mixing bowl, combine the flour, salt, and oil. Slowly add water, and knead until you're looking at a firm, smooth dough. Once achieved, cover it up and let it take a 20-minute power nap.

While our dough's dreaming of sandy beaches, let's tackle the filling. In another bowl, combine the mango, desiccated coconut, condensed milk, lime zest, and cardamom powder. Mix them up until everything's well-integrated and looking like a tropical dream.

Alright, back to our rested dough. Divide that beauty into small balls, and roll each out into a circle. Cut each circle in half. Spoon that sun-soaked filling onto one side.

Now, channel your inner samosa wizard and fold the dough over the filling, sealing the edges tight. Remember, we want all that juicy flavor trapped inside.

Fire up your frying pan with oil. When it's at that just-right temperature, introduce your samosas to the hot tub. Fry until they're sporting that golden tan. Once they're perfect, transfer them to some paper towels to take off the excess sheen.

Sprinkle those golden pockets with toasted coconut flakes. Serve them up while they're hot and let the island vibes take over. It's like a vacation in every bite. Cheers to wanderlust and culinary exploration!

Enjoy

54. Raspberry and White Chocolate Samosas

Alright, my friends, get ready to dive headfirst into a world where the tartness of raspberries meets the velvety sweetness of white chocolate. It's a dance of flavors, a tango if you will, where every bite is a mesmerizing step, leaving you begging for more.

Prep: 40 min. Cook: 20 min. Ready in: 60 min. Servings: 4

Ingredients:

For the dough:

1 cup all-purpose flour

2 tablespoons oil or ghee

A pinch of salt

Water, as needed

For the filling:

1 cup fresh raspberries

½ cup white chocolate chips

1 tablespoon granulated sugar

A dash of vanilla extract

To finish:

Oil, for frying

Powdered sugar, for dusting

Cooking Directions:

Now, down to business.

First things first, that dough of ours. In a bowl, mix together the flour, salt, and oil. Gradually add water, working the mixture till you get a solid, smooth dough. When it's all nice and firm, cover it and let it sit tight for about 20 minutes.

While our dough's chilling, let's set the stage for our main stars. In a bowl, throw in the raspberries, white chocolate chips, sugar, and vanilla extract. Mix it up, but be gentle, treat those raspberries right.

Back to our dough. Divide it into even-sized balls. Now, roll out each one into a circle. Halve it. Place a spoonful of that divine filling on one side.

Then, it's time for some samosa magic. Fold that dough over the filling, pressing the edges, making sure everything's sealed in snugly.

Next up, heat the oil in a frying pan. Once it's shimmering with anticipation, drop those samosas in. Fry them till they're beautifully golden. Once they've achieved that deep, gorgeous tan, move them to a paper towel to shed any extra oil.

Dust those crispy wonders with powdered sugar. And there you have it, folks. A dessert that's not just food, it's an emotion, an experience, a story in every bite. Dig in, and let your tastebuds travel!

Enjoy

55. Banana and Caramel Samosas

Let me paint you a picture. The comforting sweetness of bananas, combined with the seductive allure of caramel, wrapped in a crispy embrace. Sounds like a dream, doesn't it? Well, dream no more, for we're about to make that fantasy a reality.

Prep: 45 min. Cook: 20 min. Ready in: 1 h. 5 min. Servings: 4

Ingredients:

For the dough:

1 cup all-purpose flour

2 tablespoons oil or ghee

A pinch of salt

Water, as required

For the filling:

2 ripe bananas, mashed

½ cup caramel sauce

A sprinkle of cinnamon

To finish:

Oil, for frying

Desiccated coconut, for garnish

Cooking Directions:

First order of business – the dough. Combine the flour, salt, and oil in a mixing bowl. Slowly pour in water, kneading until you've got a smooth, firm dough. Once you've achieved dough nirvana, cover it and set it aside for about 20 minutes.

Meanwhile, let's whip up that filling. Mash up those bananas in a bowl till they're smooth. Pour in the caramel sauce, sprinkle in that cinnamon, and give it a gentle mix. You're looking for that harmonious melding of flavors.

Turn your attention back to the dough. Split it into equal-sized balls and roll each into a circle. Cut them in half. Load up one side with that luscious filling.

Time to fold. Bring that dough over, press the edges together, ensuring everything's sealed up tight.

Now, get that oil heated in a deep frying pan. When it's got that inviting shimmer, drop the samosas in. Fry them until they reach that glorious golden brown. Once they've achieved their best selves, take them out and let them rest on a paper towel for a moment.

Garnish with a sprinkle of desiccated coconut. And voilà! A bite of these and you're transported to a place where every moment is sweet and every memory delicious. So, pull up a chair and let's indulge.

Enjoy

56. Nutella and Hazelnut Samosas

Imagine wandering the streets of a quaint European town, taking in the sights and sounds, when suddenly the unmistakable aroma of Nutella wafts through the air. Now, add a twist to it — the warm crunch of hazelnuts. And to seal the deal, all of this goodness tucked inside a crispy samosa.

Prep: 45 min. Cook: 20 min. Ready in: 1 h. 5 min. Servings: 4

Ingredients:

For the dough:

1 cup all-purpose flour

2 tablespoons oil or ghee

A pinch of salt

Water, as required

For the filling:

½ cup Nutella

¼ cup toasted hazelnuts, chopped

A dash of vanilla extract

To finish:

Oil, for frying

Powdered sugar, for dusting

Cooking Directions:

Let's tackle that dough first. Mix together the flour, salt, and oil. Slowly add water, kneading the mixture until you're left with a smooth and firm dough. Once done, allow it to rest for about 20 minutes, covered.

While our dough's getting its beauty sleep, shift focus to our star attraction — the filling. In a bowl, blend the Nutella with those toasted hazelnuts and a hint of vanilla. Stir it up until everything's mingling nicely.

Now, back to our rested dough. Divide it into balls, rolling each into a neat circle. Halve them. It's then time to introduce each semi-circle to our Nutella mix. Spoon it on one side.

Fold. Press. Seal. Repeat. You've now got an army of samosas ready to dive into some hot oil. Fry them till they're sporting a golden-brown tan. Once done, gently place them on paper towels.

Give each one a light dusting of powdered sugar. Dive in and relish the blend of the classic European flavors with the Indian touch. Here's to the love affair between continents, one bite at a time!

Enjoy

57. Cherry and Almond Samosas

Close your eyes and imagine an orchard in summer. The sun filtering through the leaves, the scent of ripe cherries in the air, and the soft crunch of almond shells underfoot. What we're about to embark on is a journey to encapsulate that moment, that feeling, inside the crispy embrace of a samosa.

Prep: 40 min. Cook: 20 min. Ready in: 1 h. Servings: 4

Ingredients:

For the dough:

1 cup all-purpose flour

2 tablespoons oil or ghee

A pinch of salt

Water, as required

For the filling:

½ cup cherries, pitted and chopped

¼ cup toasted almonds, coarsely chopped

1 tablespoon sugar

1 teaspoon lemon zest

A touch of almond extract

To finish:

Oil, for frying

A sprinkle of toasted almond flakes

Cooking Directions:

Alright, first things first. We're making that dough. Combine your flour, salt, and oil in a bowl. Add in water bit by bit, kneading as you go, until you've got yourself a firm and smooth ball of dough. Cover it up and let it rest for about 20 minutes.

While our dough's chilling out, let's whip up a filling to rival the best desserts out there. In a bowl, toss in those juicy cherries, crunchy almonds, sugar, a zest of lemon, and that aromatic almond extract. Give it a good stir, ensuring the flavors meld well.

Returning to our well-rested dough, split it into even balls. Roll each into a circle, then halve them. On one side of each semi-circle, spoon out a generous portion of the cherry-almond mix.

Fold it over, press those edges together and seal. Keep going till you've got a battalion of samosas prepped for frying. Heat up that oil and fry these beauties until they're the perfect shade of golden brown. Once they're out, let them rest a bit on paper towels.

Before serving, give them a little sprinkle of toasted almond flakes. Voilà! A summer's day, captured within a samosa. Here's to biting into memories!

Enjoy

58. Pistachio and Rose Samosas

The bustling bazaars of the Middle East, with their vibrant colors, intoxicating scents, and the sound of distant laughter, have a way of sticking with you. This is a recipe inspired by those sensory memories. It's a rendezvous of fragrant rose and nutty pistachio – a true feast for your senses.

Prep: 45 min. Cook: 20 min. Ready in: 1 h. 5 min. Servings: 4

Ingredients:

For the dough:

1 cup all-purpose flour

2 tablespoons oil or ghee

A pinch of salt

Water, as required

For the filling:

½ cup pistachios, coarsely ground

1 tablespoon rose water

2 tablespoons sugar

A few rose petals, finely chopped

A pinch of cardamom powder

To finish:

Oil, for frying

Crushed pistachios and rose petals for garnish

Cooking Directions:

We're back at it again with our trusty dough. In a bowl, toss in your flour, salt, and oil. Gradually mix in the water, kneading until you're left with a smooth, firm ball of dough. You know the drill – cover and let it take a short nap for about 20 minutes.

While that's happening, dive into the world of filling. In another bowl, mix the ground pistachios, sugar, rose water, cardamom, and those finely chopped rose petals. It's aromatic; it's luxurious; it's what dreams are made of.

Once your dough's all refreshed and rested, divide it into even-sized balls. Roll each into a circle, and like a page from a book, split them in half. Take a semi-circle, spoon on some of that divine pistachio-rose filling onto one side, and bring it all together into a classic samosa shape. Seal those edges nice and tight.

Alright, now heat up that oil. We're frying our samosas till they're a deep, enticing golden brown. Fish them out and let them rest on paper towels for a quick minute.

Before you serve, sprinkle over some crushed pistachios and rose petals. It's an ode to a faraway land, a bite of nostalgia, right on your plate. Enjoy this fragrant journey.

Enjoy

59. Blueberry Cheesecake Samosas

I've seen my fair share of cheesecakes and savored countless blueberries, but in a samosa? Oh, this is a fusion I couldn't resist. The creaminess of the cheesecake mixed with the tartness of the blueberries, all wrapped up in that crunchy shell. Trust me; this is a bite of heaven.

Prep: 25 min. Cook: 20 min. Ready in: 45 min. Servings: 4

Ingredients:

Blueberries - 1 cup

Cream cheese - 1/2 cup

Powdered sugar - 1/4 cup

Vanilla extract - 1 tsp

Lemon zest - 1/2 tsp

For the dough:

All-purpose flour - 2 cups

Carom seeds (ajwain) - 1/2 tsp (optional)

Salt - 1/4 tsp

Ghee or unsalted butter, melted - 1/4 cup

Water - as required

Cooking Directions:

First, grab that bowl. Mix your blueberries, cream cheese, powdered sugar, vanilla extract, and lemon zest. Blend it all until it's smooth with a few chunks of blueberries for that extra burst of flavor.

Next, the dough. In a separate bowl, toss in your flour, those optional carom seeds, and salt. Pour in that melted ghee or butter, and mix it up. Slowly add water until you've got a firm dough. Knead it for a few minutes until it's smooth.

Heat up some oil in a deep-frying pan or pot. While it's getting hot, roll out your dough into circles, cut them in half, and fill them with that creamy blueberry mixture. Seal the edges.

Now, gently slide those bad boys into the hot oil. Fry them until they're golden brown.

There you have it. A dessert that'll make you question every cheesecake decision you've ever made. Dive in, savor, and let that blueberry cheesecake goodness take you to another realm.

Enjoy

60. Pineapple and Brown Sugar Samosas

The very soul of a samosa lies in its crust. Today, instead of just being a passive consumer of these tropical delights, we dive headfirst into the art of crafting that perfectly flaky dough from scratch. From raw flour to golden samosas, let's embark on this culinary journey together.

Prep: 35 min. Cook: 20 min. Ready in: 55 min. Servings: 4

Ingredients:

For the dough:

All-purpose flour, 2 cups

Water, as needed

A pinch of salt

Oil, about 2 tablespoons, plus more for frying

For the filling:

Fresh pineapple, finely chopped

Brown sugar

Ground cinnamon, a pinch

Mint leaves, for garnish (optional)

Cooking Directions:

Pour that all-purpose flour into a bowl like you're laying down a canvas. Introduce a pinch of salt to the mix. As you start adding water slowly, let your fingers dance and mingle with the ingredients. Feel the dough as it forms. There's a certain poetry in kneading, a rhythm. When it's soft but firm, add those 2 tablespoons of oil. Work it in until the dough is smooth and elastic. Let it rest for a while, letting it gather itself for the magic ahead.

While our dough takes a breather, let's address the pineapple. Mix it with brown sugar and that hint of cinnamon. It's a tropical party in a bowl, and every party needs good music, so maybe put on some tunes.

Now, back to our rested dough. Pinch off some, roll it into a small circle, ensuring it's neither too thick nor too thin. It's a delicate balance, much like life. Place a generous spoon of the pineapple mix on one half. Fold. Seal. It's like wrapping a present, every fold and crimp made with love.

Now, heat up a generous amount of oil. We're diving deep. Fry these treasures till they're golden and crispy. The aroma, the sizzle, it's like music. And when they're perfectly golden, lay them on a paper towel. They've danced in hot oil; they need a break.

You've just traveled from flour to feast, creating something that's both a treat to the eyes and the soul. And as you bite into that crisp shell, giving way to the warm, sweet, and tangy filling, remember, lives about the journey, the stories we make, the food we share. Cheers to you, the chef of the hour!

Enjoy

61. BBQ Chicken Samosas

When East meets the American South, you get a samosa that's not only flavorful but one that tells a story of cross-cultural culinary love. Today, we're infusing the spicy, smoky, and tangy notes of BBQ into the iconic Indian snack. Get ready for a rollercoaster of flavors!

Prep: 40 min. Cook: 25 min. Ready in: 1 h. 5 min. Servings: 4

Ingredients:

For the dough:

All-purpose flour, 2 cups

Water, as needed

A pinch of salt

Oil, about 2 tablespoons, plus more for frying

For the filling:

Chicken breast, finely chopped or shredded

Your favorite BBQ sauce

Red onions, finely chopped

Cheddar cheese, grated

A sprinkle of smoked paprika

Salt and pepper to taste

Cilantro, finely chopped (optional for garnish)

Cooking Directions:

First things first, grab that all-purpose flour. Pour it into a large bowl, whispering promises of the masterpiece to come. Toss in that pinch of salt, and as you begin to introduce water, knead. The dough should come alive beneath your fingers, soft yet firm, and once there, work in those tablespoons of oil. When you're done, let the dough take a well-deserved rest.

As for the filling, this is where the magic truly happens. Take your chicken – whether you've decided to chop it or shred it – and toss it with BBQ sauce until every piece sings with smoky sweetness. Stir in those red onions and the generous handful of cheddar cheese. Sprinkle with smoked paprika, salt, and pepper. Give everything one final mix, ensuring the flavors are mingling and getting to know each other.

Now, revisit your dough. Tear off a piece, roll it thin but with purpose, ensuring it can handle the weight of the story you're about to fill it with. Spoon in that BBQ chicken magic, fold, seal, and set aside.

Time to fry! Heat your oil until it's shimmering like a sunlit lake. Slide in your samosas, letting them dance and turn golden brown. Once they're gorgeously crispy, rescue them and let them rest.

For those who want an extra punch, a sprinkle of chopped cilantro will add a touch of freshness.

And there you have it — Lentil & Spinach Samosas. They're hearty, they're wholesome, and they're just waiting to be dunked into a tangy chutney or enjoyed with a side of spicy pickles. This is comfort food with a touch of elegance, a symphony in every bite.

Enjoy

62. Mexican Bean & Cheese Samosas

Imagine the bustling streets of Mumbai shaking hands with the festive vibes of Tijuana. That's what we're cooking up today. A delicious dance between Indian culinary traditions and the bold flavors of Mexican cuisine.

Prep: 40 min. Cook: 25 min. Ready in: 1 h. 5 min. Servings: 4

Ingredients:

For the dough:

All-purpose flour, 2 cups

Water, as needed

A pinch of salt

Oil, about 2 tablespoons, plus more for frying

For the filling:

Black beans, drained and rinsed

Mexican blend cheese, grated

Jalapeños, finely chopped

Cumin powder, a sprinkle

Chopped tomatoes

Chopped cilantro

Lime zest and juice

Salt and pepper to taste

A dab of sour cream for garnish (optional)

Cooking Directions:

Kick things off with the dough. Into a bowl goes your flour, laying the groundwork for what promises to be a dish for the ages. Add your salt and start introducing the water, letting your hands bring the dough to life. Once you've got that supple texture, in goes the oil. Knead it a bit more, let it rest, and turn your attention to the fiesta that'll be the filling.

In a mixing bowl, throw in those black beans, rich and earthy. To that, add the fiery burst of jalapeños, and the comforting embrace of cheese. Toss in the tomatoes, and that sprinkle of cumin, reminding us of Indian roots. Finish with cilantro, lime zest, and juice. Mix until it looks like a party in a bowl, each ingredient dancing with the others.

Now back to the dough. Tear, roll, fill, fold, and seal. You're not just making food; you're crafting memories. Stories to be told bite by bite. And then, the fry. The oil should be hot and ready, waiting to wrap your creations in a golden embrace. Once they're crisp and telling tales of two worlds meeting, pull them out, let them rest.

A dab of sour cream on each if you're feeling fancy. A touch of coolness to balance the heat.

And there you have it. Two cultures, one plate. Every bite is a journey, from the spices of India to the zest of Mexico. So, here's to the culinary tales we tell and the borders we cross, one flavorful fusion at a time. Enjoy, amigo!

Enjoy

63. Italian Meatball Samosas

Alright, imagine a cozy Italian trattoria nestled right in the busy streets of Mumbai. That's the kind of mouthwatering mashup we're diving into. Italian grandmas might be raising an eyebrow, but trust me, this blend of cultures is worth every bite.

Prep: 50 min. Cook: 30 min. Ready in: 1 h. 20 min. Servings: 4

Ingredients:

For the dough:

All-purpose flour, 2 cups

Water, as needed

A pinch of salt

Oil, about 2 tablespoons, plus more for frying

For the filling:

Ground beef, ½ pound

Breadcrumbs, ½ cup

Grated parmesan cheese, ¼ cup

Garlic, 2 cloves minced

Dried oregano, 1 teaspoon

Dried basil, 1 teaspoon

Salt and pepper to taste

Chopped tomatoes, ½ cup

Mozzarella cheese, ½ cup, shredded

Cooking Directions:

First, let's get our dough situation sorted. Flour's the main act. Into a bowl, it goes. Followed by a dash of salt. As you sprinkle in the water and knead, think of the rolling hills of Tuscany. Once you've got a smooth ball, add that oil, give it another loving knead, and let it sit there, dreaming of meatballs.

Speaking of which, let's jump to our meaty stars. Ground beef, get it in a bowl. Throw in those breadcrumbs, the sharp tang of parmesan, and the aromatic duo of garlic and herbs. Give it a good mix. Roll them into small balls, because remember, they've got to fit inside the samosas. In a skillet, brown those meatballs. Add in the chopped tomatoes, let it simmer until it's a thick sauce, and then let it cool down a bit.

Now, it's assembly time. Your dough's been resting enough. Roll it out, cut it into circles. On one half, spoon some of the meatball mixture. Sprinkle some mozzarella for that stringy cheese pull, fold over the other half, and seal the edges.

Heat up your oil. You want it hot, but not smoking. Slide in those samosas. They'll bubble, dance, and when they're golden brown and crispy, they're ready to join the party.

There you go! A bite of Italy in the heart of India. It's a crazy combination, but like most unlikely pairs, it's a match made in food heaven. As they say in Italy, "Mangia! Mangia!" or simply, "Eat! Eat!" Enjoy the fusion, my friend.

<u>Enjoy</u>

64. Greek Salad Samosas

Samosas are about to do the sirtaki with this one. We're blending the fresh flavors of a Greek salad with the crisp exterior of our favorite Indian snack. Expect Zeus to drop by for a bite.

Prep: 40 min. Cook: 25 min. Ready in: 1 h. 5 min. Servings: 4

Ingredients:

For the dough:

All-purpose flour, 2 cups

Water, as needed

A pinch of salt

Oil, about 2 tablespoons, plus more for frying

For the filling:

Cucumbers, diced, 1 cup

Cherry tomatoes, halved, 1 cup

Red onion, finely chopped, ¼ cup

Kalamata olives, pitted and chopped, ½ cup

Feta cheese, crumbled, ½ cup

Extra virgin olive oil, 2 tablespoons

Dried oregano, 1 teaspoon

Lemon zest and juice from half a lemon

Salt and pepper to taste

Cooking Directions:

Alright, let's kick things off with our dough. In goes the flour into a mixing bowl. Toss in that pinch of salt. Gradually, add water, and knead until you've got a smooth, soft dough. Now, it's time for the oil. Drizzle, knead, and then let this baby rest while we whip up some Mediterranean magic.

For our filling, it's all hands on deck. Cucumbers, cherry tomatoes, that spicy bite of red onion, and the salty goodness of Kalamata olives – they're all coming together. Mix them in a bowl. Drizzle that olive oil like you're on a Santorini sunset, sprinkle the oregano, and zest and juice that lemon like it owes you money. Give it a good toss, and then, with a grand flourish, in goes the feta. Another toss and voilà, the heart of your samosa is ready.

But let's get back to that dough. Roll it out but not too thin. Think of the pristine beaches of Mykonos. Cut it into circles, and then fill one half with that Greek salad goodness. Seal the edges and make sure it's packed tight. You don't want any of that filling to make a great escape. Your oil should be hot by now, not smoking, just eager. Gently place the samosas in, and fry them till they're golden brown and the aromas make you want to break plates in joy.

And there you have it. The Mediterranean meets the subcontinent. One bite and you're on the white-washed streets of Athens, the next, you're back on the bustling streets of Delhi. A culinary odyssey fit for the gods. Opa and namaste!

<u>Enjoy</u>

65. Thai Basil & Tofu Samosas

From the bustling streets of Bangkok to the aromatic alleys of Delhi, we're crafting a mouthwatering journey that stretches across two iconic cuisines. Get ready for a wild, flavorful ride.

Prep: 45 min. Cook: 30 min. Ready in: 1 h. 15 min. Servings: 4

Ingredients:

For the dough:

All-purpose flour, 2 cups

Water, as needed

A pinch of salt

Oil, about 2 tablespoons, plus more for frying

For the filling:

Firm tofu, cubed, 1 cup

Fresh Thai basil, chopped, ½ cup

Green chili, minced, 1

Ginger, grated, 1-inch piece

Garlic, minced, 2 cloves

Red bell pepper, finely diced, ½ cup

Soy sauce, 2 tablespoons

Brown sugar, 1 tablespoon

Lime juice, from 1 lime

Salt to taste

Cooking Directions:

First things first, our trusty samosa dough. Flour's going in, followed by salt. Mix in the water gradually, kneading until the dough starts feeling like soft playdough. Drizzle in that oil, give it another knead and set it aside, letting it dream of Thai beaches.

Now, for the flavor-packed filling. Start by heating a splash of oil in a pan. Slide in the tofu cubes and get them nice and golden. Move them around, let them catch some color, then add the ginger, garlic, and that fiery green chili. Let it sizzle and pop, then toss in the red bell pepper. The pan should be alive with color by now. Stir in the soy sauce, brown sugar, and give it a good mix. Just before turning off the heat, sprinkle in that fresh Thai basil and a squeeze of lime. Taste it, adjust the seasoning if needed, and let it cool.

Back to our dough. Roll it out into circles, not too thick, not too thin. Spoon in some of the tofu mixture on one half. Seal it, crimp the edges, and set aside.

Get that oil hot, shimmering but not smoking. Carefully lower the samosas in. Fry them up until they're beautifully golden and crisp. A tantalizing aroma should be filling the room by now.

There you have it, a culinary adventure, from the serene temples of Thailand to the vibrant streets of India. Every bite a story, every flavor a memory. Cheers to more gastronomic travels!

Enjoy

66. Korean Bulgogi Samosas

Imagine the vibrant streets of Seoul, with their tantalizing aromas and bustling energy, crashing into the ancient and mysterious alleys of Delhi. That's where we're going with these Korean Bulgogi Samosas – a culinary fusion that's bound to excite your taste buds.

Prep: 50 min. Cook: 30 min. Ready in: 1 h. 20 min. Servings: 4

Ingredients:

For the dough:

All-purpose flour, 2 cups

Water, as needed

A pinch of salt

Oil, about 2 tablespoons, plus more for frying

For the filling:

Thinly sliced beef (sirloin or ribeye), 1 cup

Soy sauce, 3 tablespoons

Brown sugar, 2 tablespoons

Sesame oil, 1 tablespoon

Garlic, minced, 3 cloves

Fresh ginger, grated, 1-inch piece

Green onions, chopped, ½ cup

Sesame seeds, 1 teaspoon

Pear or apple, grated, ½ cup (for tenderness)

Salt and pepper to taste

Cooking Directions:

Start by whisking together the soy sauce, brown sugar, sesame oil, garlic, ginger, and a generous helping of pepper. This is the marinade that's going to bring your beef to life. Add in those thinly sliced beef pieces and the grated pear or apple. Let it sit, let it soak in the magic.

Now, let's get our dough ready. Flour, salt, and water come together under your hands. Add the oil, knead until smooth, and then let it take a well-earned rest.

Back to our bulgogi. Heat a pan and throw in the marinated beef. Let it sizzle, let the sugars caramelize, and the meat brown. Once cooked, toss in those green onions and sesame seeds. Give it a good stir and take it off the heat.

Roll out the dough, fill it with the bulgogi, and seal those edges tight. Heat your oil to a shimmering dance. Fry the samosas until they're golden brown and crispy. The aroma should be transporting you straight to the heart of Seoul.

So there you have it, a blend of Korea and India in one fantastic bite. The bulgogi's sweet and savory flavors, locked within a crisp samosa, are a testament to the beautiful chaos of culinary fusion.

Enjoy

67. Mediterranean Hummus & Veggie Samosas

Picture the sun-drenched shores of the Mediterranean meeting the vibrant markets of Mumbai. We're taking a classic Indian snack and giving it a refreshing Mediterranean twist with hummus and an array of fresh veggies. This one's like a sunny day for your palate.

Prep: 45 min. Cook: 30 min. Ready in: 1 h. 15 min. Servings: 4

Ingredients:

For the dough:

All-purpose flour, 2 cups

Water, as needed

A pinch of salt

Oil, about 2 tablespoons, plus more for frying

For the filling:

Hummus, 1 cup

Spinach, chopped, ½ cup

Sun-dried tomatoes, chopped, ¼ cup

Kalamata olives, pitted and chopped, ¼ cup

Feta cheese, crumbled, ½ cup

Red onion, finely chopped, ¼ cup

Dried oregano, 1 teaspoon

Lemon zest, 1 teaspoon

Salt and pepper to taste

Cooking Directions:

Begin with the dough, as always. Flour dances into the bowl, joined by a pinch of salt. As you add water and start kneading, think of the rolling Mediterranean waves. Add the oil, knead until smooth, and let it rest, contemplating the flavors about to come.

For the filling, it's all about freshness and zest. Mix together that creamy hummus, spinach, sun-dried tomatoes, Kalamata olives, crumbled feta, and red onion. Sprinkle in the oregano, lemon zest, and a bit of salt and pepper. Each ingredient is like a piece of a Mediterranean mosaic.

Now, roll out the dough, not too thick, not too thin. Fill each circle with a spoonful of the hummus mixture. Fold, seal, and repeat.

In a hot pan, let the oil get excited. Slide in your samosas and watch them turn a beautiful golden brown. They should be crispy, the insides warm and bursting with flavor.

There you have it, a culinary voyage from the heart of India to the soul of the Mediterranean. Each bite is a blend of cultures, a celebration of flavors. So sit back, savor each bite, and let your taste buds do the traveling.

Enjoy

68. American Cheeseburger Samosas

Imagine the classic American cheeseburger crashing an Indian street food party. That's exactly what we're cooking up today. It's a playful, delicious twist on two culinary giants: the all-American cheeseburger and the ever-popular Indian samosa.

Prep: 50 min. Cook: 30 min. Ready in: 1 h. 20 min. Servings: 4

Ingredients:

For the dough:

All-purpose flour, 2 cups

Water, as needed

A pinch of salt

Oil, about 2 tablespoons, plus more for frying

For the filling:

Ground beef, 1 cup

Onion, finely chopped, ¼ cup

Garlic, minced, 1 clove

Cheddar cheese, grated, ½ cup

Pickles, finely chopped, ¼ cup

Mustard, 1 tablespoon

Ketchup, 1 tablespoon

Salt and pepper to taste

Cooking Directions:

Let's get started with our dough. Flour, salt, and water come together in a bowl. Mix and knead until you have a smooth, pliable dough. Drizzle in the oil, give it one last knead, and let it sit. It's like setting the stage for our star performers.

Now, let's tackle the filling. Cook up that ground beef in a pan. Add the onions, garlic, and cook until the beef is nicely browned. Let it be the base of our cheeseburger narrative. Then, introduce the cheddar cheese, pickles, a dab of mustard, and ketchup. Stir it well, adding a bit of salt and pepper. Let this filling cool, combining the classic burger elements.

Roll out the dough, and cut it into circles. Spoon a portion of the cheeseburger mixture onto each piece. Fold, seal, and make sure it's packed nicely.

Heat up a good amount of oil. When it's hot enough, carefully drop in the samosas. Fry them to a perfect golden brown. They should be crispy on the outside, with that comforting cheeseburger goodness on the inside.

And there you have it: an American classic in an Indian avatar. Each bite is a playful journey between cultures, a delicious melding of East and West. It's a fun, unexpected twist that's sure to delight your taste buds.

Enjoy

69. Chinese Sweet and Sour Pork Samosas

Sometimes, the simplest of ingredients come together to form a gastronomic orchestra. Today, we're looking at two rock stars of the vegetarian world: lentils and spinach. Together in a samosa, they're a bit like a folk duo — earthy, soulful, and immensely satisfying.

Prep: 55 min. Cook: 35 min. Ready in: 1 h. 30 min. Servings: 4

Ingredients:

For the dough:

All-purpose flour, 2 cups
Water, as needed
A pinch of salt
Oil, about 2 tablespoons, plus more for frying

For the filling:

Pork tenderloin, finely chopped, 1 cup
Bell peppers (a mix of colors), finely chopped, ½ cup
Pineapple, finely chopped, ¼ cup
Soy sauce, 2 tablespoons
Rice vinegar, 1 tablespoon
Brown sugar, 2 tablespoons
Garlic, minced, 1 clove
Ginger, minced, 1 teaspoon
Cornstarch, 1 teaspoon
Water, 2 tablespoons
Green onions, finely chopped, for garnish
Sesame seeds, for garnish

Cooking Directions:

First, let's get our samosa dough ready. Flour, salt, water – mix and knead until it's soft and obedient under your fingers. Add the oil, give it another good knead, then let it take a short nap.

Now, the filling. In a pan, let the pork sizzle and brown. Add in those colorful bell peppers, the pineapple for a touch of sweetness, and then garlic and ginger for that essential zing. In a small bowl, whisk together soy sauce, rice vinegar, brown sugar, and cornstarch dissolved in water. Pour this over the pork, letting it coat the pieces in a glossy, sticky sauce. Once it thickens, remove from heat and let it cool.

Roll out your dough, nice and even. Spoon a bit of that sweet and sour pork onto each piece, fold, and seal. These little parcels are ready for their hot oil bath.

Fry them till they're golden, crispy, and utterly irresistible. Drain on a paper towel.

Serve these golden beauties hot, garnished with some green onions and a sprinkle of sesame seeds. It's East meets East in a festival of flavors. Each bite is a journey through continents, a celebration of fusion cuisine at its best.

Enjoy

70. Japanese Teriyaki Chicken Samosas

Imagine a tranquil Japanese garden, cherry blossoms in bloom, merging with the vibrant chaos of an Indian street. That's the essence we're capturing in these Japanese Teriyaki Chicken Samosas – a delightful mix of subtlety and spice, serenity and excitement.

Prep: 50 min. Cook: 30 min. Ready in: 1 h. 20 min. Servings: 4

Ingredients:

For the dough:

All-purpose flour, 2 cups

Water, as needed

A pinch of salt

Oil, about 2 tablespoons, plus more for frying

For the filling:

Chicken breast, finely chopped, 1 cup

Soy sauce, 3 tablespoons

Mirin, 2 tablespoons

Brown sugar, 1 tablespoon

Garlic, minced, 1 clove

Ginger, minced, 1 teaspoon

Spring onions, finely chopped, ¼ cup

Sesame seeds, for garnish

Cooking Directions:

Let's start with our dough. Flour, salt, and water come together in a harmonious blend. Knead it well, add the oil, and let it rest, dreaming of far-off lands.

For the filling, let's bring Japan into our kitchen. In a pan, cook the chicken until it's nearly done. Then, add the soy sauce, mirin, and brown sugar. Let these flavors mingle with the chicken, adding garlic and ginger for that punch. The sauce should thicken, coating the chicken in a glossy, sticky glaze. Throw in some spring onions at the end for freshness.

Roll out the dough, and cut it into circles. Place a spoonful of the teriyaki chicken in the center of each, fold, and seal. These samosas are now little parcels of cross-continental love.

Heat the oil. It's time for these beauties to get their golden tan. Fry them until they are the color of a Japanese autumn – crisp and inviting. Drain them on a paper towel.

Serve these samosas hot, sprinkled with sesame seeds. Each bite takes you on a journey – from the bustling streets of Delhi to the peaceful, cherry-blossomed landscapes of Japan. It's more than a meal; it's a cultural symphony.

Enjoy

71. Tofu and Veggie Stir Fry Samosas

We're taking a trip to the heart of a bustling Asian marketplace and then zipping over to the lively streets of Mumbai. These Tofu & Veggie Stir Fry Samosas are all about vibrant colors, crunchy textures, and flavors that sing with freshness.

Prep: 45 min. Cook: 30 min. Ready in: 1 h. 15 min. Servings: 4

Ingredients:

For the dough:

All-purpose flour, 2 cups

Water, as needed

A pinch of salt

Oil, about 2 tablespoons, plus more for frying

For the filling:

Firm tofu, pressed and cubed, 1 cup

Mixed vegetables (carrots, bell peppers, snap peas), finely chopped, 1 cup

Soy sauce, 2 tablespoons

Sesame oil, 1 teaspoon

Garlic, minced, 2 cloves

Ginger, minced, 1-inch piece

Green onion, chopped, for garnish

Sesame seeds, for garnish

Cooking Directions:

First up, our dough. Flour, salt, and water. Mix and knead until it's a smooth, supple ball of potential. Drizzle in the oil, give it another good knead, and let it rest while we turn our attention to the stir fry.

Heat a splash of sesame oil in a pan. Toss in the tofu cubes. We want them golden and crispy on the outside. Next, add those colorful veggies. Stir them around until they start to soften but still retain some crunch. Now, in goes the garlic and ginger for that aromatic kick. Splash in the soy sauce and let everything cook together for a few more minutes. This is the filling that's going to make our samosas stand out. Roll out the dough into circles. Spoon in your tofu and veggie mix, fold, and crimp the edges. These are ready for their hot oil debut.

Get the oil nice and hot. Fry the samosas until they're golden brown and crispy. The sound of sizzling samosas should be music to your ears.

Serve these hot, garnished with green onions and a sprinkle of sesame seeds. They're a festival of textures and flavors, a fusion that spans continents. It's like taking a culinary journey with every bite.

Enjoy

72. Chickpea & Spinach Samosas

Embark on a culinary adventure that melds the hearty, earthy flavors of chickpeas with the fresh, vibrant taste of spinach, all packed in a delightful Indian samosa. It's a vegetarian dream, a fusion that's both nourishing and incredibly tasty.

Prep: 45 min. Cook: 30 min. Ready in: 1 h. 15 min. Servings: 4

Ingredients:

For the dough:

All-purpose flour, 2 cups

Water, as needed

A pinch of salt

Oil, about 2 tablespoons, plus more for frying

For the filling:

Chickpeas, cooked and mashed, 1 cup

Spinach, finely chopped, 1 cup

Onion, finely chopped, ¼ cup

Garlic, minced, 2 cloves

Ground cumin, 1 teaspoon

Coriander powder, 1 teaspoon

Garam masala, ½ teaspoon

Lemon juice, 1 tablespoon

Salt and pepper to taste

Cooking Directions:

First, let's get that dough going. Flour, salt, and water come together in a beautiful ballet under your hands. Once it's a smooth ball, add the oil and let it rest, dreaming of the flavors to come.

Now, the heart of our samosa – the filling. In a bowl, mash those chickpeas. They should be soft but with some texture left. To this, add the chopped spinach, onion, and all those spices – cumin, coriander, garam masala. It's like a tour through an Indian spice market. Finish it with a squeeze of lemon juice, and a bit of salt and pepper.

Roll out your dough, nice and thin. Each circle gets a generous helping of the chickpea mixture. Fold, seal, and they're ready for their hot oil bath.

Fry these beauties until they're golden brown, crispy on the outside, with a burst of flavor on the inside. Drain them on a paper towel.

Serve these hot, with a side of mint chutney or tamarind sauce. Each bite takes you through a journey of textures and flavors – from the comforting earthiness of chickpeas to the fresh zing of spinach. It's a vegetarian feast that's sure to please everyone at the table.

Enjoy

73. Vegan "Cheese" & Onion Samosas

We're breaking the mold and diving into a vegan delight. These Vegan "Cheese" & Onion Samosas merge the classic comfort of melted cheese and onion with a vegan twist. It's a modern take on a traditional favorite, perfect for anyone looking to indulge in plant-based goodness.

Prep: 50 min. Cook: 30 min. Ready in: 1 h. 20 min. Servings: 4

Ingredients:

For the dough:

All-purpose flour, 2 cups

Water, as needed

A pinch of salt

Oil, about 2 tablespoons, plus more for frying

For the filling:

Vegan cheese, grated, 1 cup

Onion, finely chopped, ½ cup

Garlic, minced, 1 clove

Paprika, ½ teaspoon

Salt and pepper to taste

Fresh parsley, chopped, for garnish

Cooking Directions:

First up, we're crafting our dough. Flour finds its way into a bowl, joined by a pinch of salt. Gradually add water as you knead, aiming for a dough that's smooth and elastic. Once you've achieved that, work in the oil and let the dough rest, gathering its strength.

For the filling, it's simplicity at its finest. Mix together the vegan cheese and finely chopped onion. Add a touch of garlic, a hint of paprika, and season with salt and pepper. It's a filling that speaks of cozy evenings and warm hearts.

Now, roll out that dough into even circles. Spoon a portion of the vegan cheese and onion mixture onto each, fold, and seal with a promise of deliciousness.

Heat your oil, ready for frying. These samosas want to turn golden brown, achieving that perfect crunch. When they're ready, let them take a moment on a paper towel.

Serve these hot, perhaps with a sprinkle of fresh parsley on top. Each bite is a revelation – who knew vegan could taste so good? It's a testament to the power of simplicity and the joy of plant-based cooking. Enjoy the melding of flavors and the breaking of boundaries.

Enjoy

74. Seitan & BBQ Sauce Samosas

Imagine a smoky BBQ joint tucked away in the busy streets of an Indian city. That's the essence we're capturing in these Seitan & BBQ Sauce Samosas – a fusion that's daring, bold, and oh-so-satisfying, especially for those who love a meaty texture without the meat.

Prep: 50 min. Cook: 30 min. Ready in: 1 h. 20 min. Servings: 4

Ingredients:

For the dough:

All-purpose flour, 2 cups

Water, as needed

A pinch of salt

Oil, about 2 tablespoons, plus more for frying

For the filling:

Seitan, finely chopped, 1 cup

Your favorite BBQ sauce, ¼ cup

Onion, finely chopped, ¼ cup

Garlic, minced, 1 clove

Smoked paprika, ½ teaspoon

Cumin, ½ teaspoon

Salt and pepper to taste

Fresh cilantro, chopped, for garnish

Cooking Directions:

Start with the dough. Flour takes center stage in a bowl, joined by salt. Add water slowly, kneading until you have a soft, pliable dough. Introduce the oil, knead it in, then set the dough aside to rest while you concoct the filling.

For the filling, seitan is your star. Fry it up until it's crispy and browned. Then mix in the onions, and let them soften. Add garlic, smoked paprika, and cumin for that deep, smoky flavor. Pour in the BBQ sauce and let everything come together, simmering gently. Season with salt and pepper.

Now, back to your dough. Roll it out, cut into circles, and fill each one with a spoonful of the seitan mixture. Fold, seal, and they're ready for the fryer.

In hot oil, cook these samosas until they're golden brown and temptingly crisp. They should sizzle their way to perfection. Drain them on a paper towel.

Serve them piping hot, garnished with a sprinkle of fresh cilantro. These samosas are a celebration of flavor, a nod to BBQ lovers, and a wink to those who love their food with a bit of an edge. It's a culinary fusion that's sure to delight and surprise.

Enjoy

75. Tempeh & Broccoli Samosas

Brace yourselves for a samosa that's not just a snack, it's a statement. We're pairing the nutty, hearty flavors of tempeh with the fresh crunch of broccoli, creating a fusion that's as nutritious as it is delicious. Welcome to the world of Tempeh & Broccoli Samosas.

Prep: 50 min. Cook: 30 min. Ready in: 1 h. 20 min. Servings: 4

Ingredients:

For the dough:

All-purpose flour, 2 cups

Water, as needed

A pinch of salt

Oil, about 2 tablespoons, plus more for frying

For the filling:

Tempeh, crumbled, 1 cup

Broccoli, finely chopped, 1 cup

Soy sauce, 2 tablespoons

Sesame oil, 1 teaspoon

Garlic, minced, 2 cloves

Ginger, minced, 1 teaspoon

Red chili flakes, ½ teaspoon

Green onions, finely chopped, ¼ cup

Sesame seeds, for garnish

Cooking Directions:

First, let's tackle the dough. Flour, salt, and water will be our foundation. Knead them together, adding water gradually until you get a smooth, elastic dough. Mix in the oil, give it a final knead, and let it rest, dreaming of the flavors it will soon embrace.

Now, the filling. Heat up that sesame oil in a pan. Toss in the crumbled tempeh – you want it to get a bit of color, a bit of character. Then, in go the broccoli, garlic, and ginger. Stir it around until the broccoli is bright and slightly tender. Splash in the soy sauce and sprinkle the red chili flakes for that kick. Once it's all beautifully combined and fragrant, take it off the heat.

Roll out the dough and cut it into circles. Each piece gets a spoonful of your tempeh and broccoli mix. Fold, seal, and prepare them for their crispy fate.

In a hot pool of oil, fry these samosas until they're golden brown and irresistibly crunchy. Drain them on a paper towel.

Serve these samosas hot, sprinkled with sesame seeds and maybe a side of spicy dipping sauce. It's a bite that brings together the best of multiple worlds – the earthy goodness of tempeh, the freshness of broccoli, all wrapped in a classic Indian package.

Enjoy

76. Vegan "Chicken" & Mushroom Samosas

Today, we're bridging the gap between traditional Indian flavors and modern vegan cuisine. These Vegan "Chicken" & Mushroom Samosas are a nod to classic tastes while embracing the innovative world of plant-based alternatives. Get ready for a symphony of flavors wrapped in a crispy, golden crust.

Prep: 55 min. Cook: 35 min. Ready in: 1 h. 30 min. Servings: 4

Ingredients:

For the dough:

All-purpose flour, 2 cups

Water, as needed

A pinch of salt

Oil, about 2 tablespoons, plus more for frying

For the filling:

Vegan chicken substitute, chopped, 1 cup

Mushrooms, finely chopped, 1 cup

Onion, finely chopped, ¼ cup

Garlic, minced, 2 cloves

Thyme, 1 teaspoon

Soy sauce, 1 tablespoon

Vegan cream or coconut milk, ¼ cup

Salt and pepper to taste

Fresh parsley, chopped, for garnish

Cooking Directions:

Begin with the dough. Flour in the bowl, add a pinch of salt. As you pour in the water and start kneading, let the rhythm take over until you have a soft, pliable dough. Introduce the oil, knead it in, then let the dough rest while you conjure up the filling.

For the filling, let's get a pan hot. Add the vegan chicken pieces, let them brown slightly, then introduce the mushrooms. As they cook down, add the onions, garlic, and thyme, infusing the mix with aromatic goodness. Splash in the soy sauce for depth, and then add the vegan cream or coconut milk to bring everything together into a creamy, luscious filling. Season with salt and pepper.

Now, the assembly. Roll out the dough, cut it into circles, spoon the filling onto each piece, fold, and seal. These parcels are now ready for their hot oil journey.

Fry them till they're golden brown and crispy. The sound of sizzling should be filling your kitchen with anticipation.

Serve these samosas hot, garnished with a sprinkle of fresh parsley. It's a dish that's not just satisfying in flavor but also in its ethos – a perfect choice for the conscious gourmet. Each bite is a celebration of how delicious and diverse vegan cuisine can be.

Enjoy

77. Jackfruit & Curry Samosas

Embrace a taste of tropical India with these Jackfruit & Curry Samosas. We're combining the meaty texture of jackfruit with rich, aromatic spices to create a vegan delight that's both hearty and flavor-packed. These samosas are a testament to the versatility and richness of plant-based cuisine.

Prep: 55 min. Cook: 35 min. Ready in: 1 h. 30 min. Servings: 4

Ingredients:

For the dough:

All-purpose flour, 2 cups
Water, as needed
A pinch of salt
Oil, about 2 tablespoons, plus more for frying

For the filling:

Young green jackfruit (canned or fresh), drained and shredded, 1 cup
Onion, finely chopped, ¼ cup
Garlic, minced, 2 cloves
Ginger, minced, 1-inch piece
Ground turmeric, ½ teaspoon
Ground cumin, 1 teaspoon
Ground coriander, 1 teaspoon
Garam masala, ½ teaspoon
Tomato paste, 2 tablespoons
Coconut milk, ¼ cup
Fresh cilantro, chopped, for garnish
Salt and pepper to taste

Cooking Directions:

Let's start with our dough. Flour, salt, and water mix together in a bowl. Knead it until you've got a smooth dough. Drizzle in the oil, give it another good knead, then let it take a break while you create the filling.

For the filling, heat a pan, and sauté the onions until they're soft. Add the garlic, ginger, turmeric, cumin, coriander, and garam masala. Let the spices bloom with their fragrant aromas. Stir in the jackfruit, mixing well to coat it with the spices. Add the tomato paste and coconut milk, and let it simmer until the mixture thickens. Season with salt and pepper.

Now, roll out your dough, cut into circles. Place a spoonful of the jackfruit curry onto each, fold, and seal them up, ready for their hot oil dip.

Fry these samosas in oil until they're golden brown, crispy, and utterly irresistible. Drain them on a paper towel.

Serve these flavorful parcels hot, garnished with fresh cilantro. It's a dish that brings a tropical twist to the traditional samosa, showcasing the wonders of vegan cooking. Dive in and enjoy the blend of textures and flavors that make this dish a memorable culinary adventure.

Enjoy

78. Lentil & Carrot Samosas

Join me on a culinary journey where the humble lentil meets the sweet earthiness of carrots, all wrapped in a crisp samosa shell. These Lentil & Carrot Samosas are a celebration of simple, nourishing ingredients, coming together to create something truly special.

Prep: 50 min. Cook: 30 min. Ready in: 1 h. 20 min. Servings: 4

Ingredients:

For the dough:

All-purpose flour, 2 cups

Water, as needed

A pinch of salt

Oil, about 2 tablespoons, plus more for frying

For the filling:

Red lentils, cooked and drained, 1 cup

Carrots, finely grated, ½ cup

Onion, finely chopped, ¼ cup

Garlic, minced, 2 cloves

Ground cumin, 1 teaspoon

Ground coriander, 1 teaspoon

Chili powder, ½ teaspoon

Fresh cilantro, chopped, for garnish

Salt and pepper to taste

Cooking Directions:

Begin with the dough. Combine flour, salt, and water in a bowl, kneading until you have a smooth and elastic dough. Work in the oil, then let it rest, allowing the gluten to relax.

For the filling, let's get those lentils and carrots ready. In a pan, sauté the onions until translucent. Add the garlic, cumin, coriander, and chili powder, letting the spices release their aromas. Stir in the cooked lentils and grated carrots, mixing well. Cook until the mixture is dry, then season with salt and pepper. Let it cool a bit before using.

Now, roll out the dough into thin circles. Place a spoonful of the lentil mixture on one side, fold over, and seal the edges. Ensure they are well sealed to prevent any filling from escaping during frying.

Heat oil in a deep-frying pan. Once hot, carefully slide in the samosas and fry until golden brown and crispy. They should sizzle their way to perfection. Drain on paper towels.

Serve these hearty samosas hot, garnished with fresh cilantro. They're a testament to the beauty of simple, vegan cooking – nourishing, flavorful, and satisfying. A perfect snack for any time of day, bringing a touch of Indian flavor to your table.

Enjoy

79. Vegan "Beef" & Peppers Samosas

Embrace a fusion of bold flavors with these Vegan "Beef" & Peppers Samosas. We're combining the hearty texture of vegan beef with the sweetness of bell peppers, all wrapped in a crispy, golden crust. It's a dish that's both comforting and exciting, perfect for vegans and meat-lovers alike.

Prep: 55 min. Cook: 35 min. Ready in: 1 h. 30 min. Servings: 4

Ingredients:

For the dough:

All-purpose flour, 2 cups
Water, as needed
A pinch of salt
Oil, about 2 tablespoons, plus more for frying

For the filling:

Vegan beef substitute, crumbled, 1 cup
Bell peppers (red and green), finely chopped, ½ cup
Onion, finely chopped, ¼ cup
Garlic, minced, 2 cloves
Cumin, ½ teaspoon
Smoked paprika, ½ teaspoon
Chili powder, ½ teaspoon
Tomato paste, 1 tablespoon
Salt and pepper to taste
Fresh parsley or cilantro, chopped, for garnish

Cooking Directions:

Let's begin with our dough. Mix flour and salt in a bowl. Gradually add water, kneading until you have a soft, elastic dough. Add the oil, give it another good knead, and let it rest.

For the filling, heat up a pan. Add the vegan beef substitute, cooking it until it starts to brown. Toss in the onions, bell peppers, and garlic, cooking until they're soft. Now, let's spice it up with cumin, smoked paprika, and chili powder. Stir in the tomato paste, season with salt and pepper, and let the mixture cook down until it's flavorful and slightly thickened.

Now, roll out your dough into thin circles. Spoon the vegan beef and pepper mixture onto one side, fold, and seal them tightly.

In hot oil, fry these samosas until they're crispy and golden brown. The aroma should be tantalizing by now.

Serve these piping hot, garnished with fresh parsley or cilantro. Every bite packs a punch of robust flavor, making these samosas a fantastic treat for any gathering. Dive in and enjoy the delightful blend of textures and tastes that make this dish truly unique.

Enjoy

80. Mushroom & Vegan "Cheese" Samosas

Imagine a cozy, earthy forest glade meeting the vibrant bustle of an Indian street market. That's the essence of these Mushroom & Vegan "Cheese" Samosas – a culinary fusion that brings together the deep, umami flavors of mushrooms with the creamy richness of vegan cheese, all enclosed in a crispy samosa shell.

Prep: 50 min. Cook: 30 min. Ready in: 1 h. 20 min. Servings: 4

Ingredients:

For the dough:

All-purpose flour, 2 cups

Water, as needed

A pinch of salt

Oil, about 2 tablespoons, plus more for frying

For the filling:

Mushrooms, finely chopped, 1 cup

Vegan cheese, grated, ½ cup

Garlic, minced, 2 cloves

Onion, finely chopped, ¼ cup

Thyme, 1 teaspoon

Soy sauce, 1 tablespoon

Salt and pepper to taste

Fresh parsley, chopped, for garnish

Cooking Directions:

First, we make the dough. Combine the flour and salt in a bowl, and then gradually add water, kneading into a smooth dough. Work in the oil, knead it a bit more, and let it rest. This dough is the foundation of our flavorful journey.

Now, for the filling. Sauté the onions and garlic until they're soft and fragrant. Add the mushrooms, letting them cook down and release their moisture. Stir in thyme and soy sauce, infusing our mixture with an umami depth. Finally, mix in the vegan cheese, letting it melt slightly. Season with salt and pepper.

Roll out the dough into thin circles. Place a spoonful of the mushroom and vegan cheese mixture on one side, fold, and seal the edges, ensuring no filling can escape.

Heat oil in a frying pan. Once hot, fry the samosas until they turn a beautiful golden brown, crispy and tempting.

Serve these hot, garnished with chopped parsley. These Mushroom & Vegan "Cheese" Samosas are a testament to the power of plant-based ingredients, creating a dish that's both indulgent and wholesome. Each bite is a celebration of flavors and textures, sure to delight vegans and non-vegans alike.

Enjoy

81. Quinoa & Veggie Samosas

Embrace a healthier twist on the traditional samosa with these Quinoa & Veggie Samosas. We're combining the nutty goodness of quinoa with a medley of fresh vegetables, all wrapped in a gluten-free pastry. It's a dish that's as nutritious as it is delicious, perfect for those seeking a lighter, yet satisfying, snack.

Prep: 55 min. Cook: 35 min. Ready in: 1 h. 30 min. Servings: 4

Ingredients:

For the dough:

Gluten-free all-purpose flour, 2 cups

Water, as needed

A pinch of salt

Oil, about 2 tablespoons, plus more for frying

For the filling:

Quinoa, cooked, 1 cup

Mixed vegetables (carrots, peas, corn), finely chopped, 1 cup

Onion, finely chopped, ¼ cup

Garlic, minced, 1 clove

Cumin powder, 1 teaspoon

Coriander powder, 1 teaspoon

Fresh cilantro, chopped, for garnish

Salt and pepper to taste

Cooking Directions:

Start with the dough. In a bowl, mix gluten-free flour and salt. Gradually add water, kneading until you've got a soft, pliable dough. Drizzle in the oil, give it a final knead, and let it rest. This gluten-free dough is the heart of our healthier samosas.

For the filling, let's get those veggies going. Sauté the onions and garlic until they're soft. Add the mixed vegetables, cooked quinoa, cumin, and coriander powder. Stir well, letting the spices marry with the quinoa and veggies. Season with salt and pepper. Let it cool slightly before using.

Now, roll out the dough into thin circles. Spoon a portion of the quinoa mixture onto each, fold, and seal the edges. These parcels are ready for their crispy transformation.

Heat oil in a deep frying pan. Once hot, gently lower the samosas in and fry until golden brown and crispy. Drain on paper towels.

Serve these delightful Quinoa & Veggie Samosas hot, garnished with fresh cilantro. They're a celebration of health and flavor, showcasing that eating well doesn't mean sacrificing taste. Enjoy the burst of nutrients and flavors, wrapped in a crispy, golden crust.

Enjoy

82. Brown Rice & Chicken Samosas

Imagine a fusion where the wholesomeness of brown rice meets the comforting richness of chicken, all encased in a gluten-free samosa. That's what we're creating with these Brown Rice & Chicken Samosas – a hearty, flavorful snack that's both satisfying and sensitive to dietary needs.

Prep: 60 min. Cook: 40 min. Ready in: 1 h. 40 min. Servings: 4

Ingredients:

For the dough:

Gluten-free all-purpose flour, 2 cups

Water, as needed

A pinch of salt

Oil, about 2 tablespoons, plus more for frying

For the filling:

Brown rice, cooked, 1 cup

Chicken breast, cooked and shredded, 1 cup

Onion, finely chopped, ¼ cup

Garlic, minced, 1 clove

Cumin powder, 1 teaspoon

Paprika, ½ teaspoon

Green peas, ½ cup

Fresh parsley or cilantro, chopped, for garnish

Salt and pepper to taste

Cooking Directions:

Begin with the dough. In a large bowl, whisk together gluten-free flour and salt. Gradually add water, kneading until a soft, elastic dough forms. Work in the oil, then let the dough rest. This gluten-free base will crisply encase our nutritious filling.

For the filling, heat a pan and sauté the onions and garlic until they're aromatic and tender. Add the cooked chicken, brown rice, cumin, and paprika. Toss in the green peas for a pop of color and flavor. Stir everything together until well combined. Season with salt and pepper, then set aside to cool.

Roll out the dough into thin, even circles. Spoon the chicken and rice mixture onto one side of each circle, fold, and seal the edges securely. Heat oil in a deep frying pan. Once it's hot, carefully place the samosas in the oil and fry them until they are golden brown and crispy. Drain them on paper towels.

Serve these Brown Rice & Chicken Samosas hot, garnished with fresh parsley or cilantro. They're a perfect blend of heartiness and health, offering a delicious way to enjoy a classic snack without the gluten. Each bite is a testament to the versatility and delicious possibilities of gluten-free cooking.

Enjoy

83. Potato & Beef Samosas

We're taking a classic comfort food pairing and giving it a twist in these Potato & Beef Samosas. Imagine the heartiness of mashed potatoes combined with savory ground beef, all enveloped in a gluten-free samosa pastry. It's a match made in culinary heaven, perfect for a satisfying snack or a hearty appetizer.

Prep: 60 min. Cook: 40 min. Ready in: 1 h. 40 min. Servings: 4

Ingredients:

For the dough:

Gluten-free all-purpose flour, 2 cups

Water, as needed

A pinch of salt

Oil, about 2 tablespoons, plus more for frying

For the filling:

Potatoes, boiled and mashed, 1 cup

Ground beef, cooked and drained, 1 cup

Onion, finely chopped, ¼ cup

Garlic, minced, 1 clove

Ground cumin, 1 teaspoon

Ground coriander, ½ teaspoon

Chili powder, ½ teaspoon

Fresh cilantro, chopped, for garnish

Salt and pepper to taste

Cooking Directions:

Start with the dough. Mix the gluten-free flour and salt in a large bowl. Gradually add water, kneading until you have a soft, pliable dough. Add the oil and knead it a bit more, then let it rest.

For the filling, in a pan, sauté the onions and garlic until they're soft and fragrant. Add the cooked ground beef, mixing it well with the onions. Stir in the mashed potatoes, cumin, coriander, and chili powder, and cook everything together until it's well combined and flavorful. Season with salt and pepper.

Now, roll out the dough into thin, even circles. Place a spoonful of the potato and beef mixture onto one side of each circle, fold, and seal the edges well.

Heat oil in a deep frying pan. Once it's hot, fry the samosas in batches until they are golden brown and crispy. Drain them on paper towels.

Serve these Potato & Beef Samosas hot, garnished with fresh cilantro. They offer a comforting and familiar flavor in a unique gluten-free package. Perfect for a cozy night in or as a crowd-pleasing appetizer, these samosas are sure to satisfy any savory craving.

Enjoy

84. Chickpea Flour & Lamb Samosas

Embark on a culinary journey with these Chickpea Flour & Lamb Samosas, where the rich and savory flavors of lamb meet the nutty, wholesome goodness of chickpea flour. This gluten-free twist on the classic samosa is a delightful fusion, offering a robust taste experience.

Prep: 30 min. Cook: 35 min. Ready in: 1 h. 5 min. Servings: 4

Ingredients:

For the dough:

Chickpea flour (Besan), 2 cups

Water, as needed

A pinch of salt

Oil, about 2 tablespoons, plus more for frying

For the filling:

Ground lamb, cooked and drained, 1 cup

Onion, finely chopped, ¼ cup

Garlic, minced, 1 clove

Fresh ginger, minced, 1-inch piece

Garam masala, 1 teaspoon

Ground cumin, ½ teaspoon

Chopped tomatoes, ½ cup

Fresh mint, chopped, for garnish

Salt and pepper to taste

Cooking Directions:

Begin with the dough. In a bowl, combine chickpea flour and salt. Add water gradually, kneading to form a smooth, pliable dough. Work in the oil, knead again, and let it rest, allowing the flavors to meld.

For the filling, cook the ground lamb in a pan until it's nicely browned. Add the onions, garlic, and ginger, cooking until the onions are soft. Sprinkle in the garam masala and cumin, stirring well. Add the chopped tomatoes and cook until the mixture is rich and thickened. Season with salt and pepper.

Now, roll out the dough into thin circles. Spoon the lamb mixture onto one half of each circle, fold over, and seal the edges securely.

In a deep-frying pan, heat the oil. Fry the samosas until they are golden brown and crispy, ensuring they cook evenly on all sides. Drain them on paper towels.

Serve these Chickpea Flour & Lamb Samosas hot, garnished with fresh mint. They're a perfect blend of hearty lamb and the unique taste of chickpea flour, making them a standout gluten-free snack or appetizer. Savor the rich flavors and enjoy the delightful textures that make this dish a memorable treat.

Enjoy

85. Lentil & Spinach Samosas

We're taking a healthful turn with these Lentil & Spinach Samosas, blending the earthy flavors of lentils with the fresh, green taste of spinach. Wrapped in a gluten-free crust, these samosas are a perfect blend of nutrition and flavor, ideal for those seeking a wholesome yet delicious snack.

Prep: 50 min. Cook: 30 min. Ready in: 1 h. 20 min. Servings: 4

Ingredients:

For the dough:

Gluten-free all-purpose flour, 2 cups

Water, as needed

A pinch of salt

Oil, about 2 tablespoons, plus more for frying

For the filling:

Red or green lentils, cooked and drained, 1 cup

Spinach, finely chopped, 1 cup

Onion, finely chopped, ¼ cup

Garlic, minced, 2 cloves

Ground cumin, 1 teaspoon

Ground coriander, ½ teaspoon

Chili powder, ½ teaspoon

Lemon juice, 1 tablespoon

Fresh cilantro, chopped, for garnish

Salt and pepper to taste

Cooking Directions:

Let's begin with the dough. In a large mixing bowl, combine gluten-free flour and a pinch of salt. Gradually add water and knead until a smooth, elastic dough forms. Add the oil and knead it a bit more, then set it aside to rest.

For the filling, sauté the onions and garlic in a pan until they're translucent and fragrant. Stir in the cooked lentils and spinach, cooking until the spinach wilts and the flavors meld. Season with cumin, coriander, chili powder, lemon juice, salt, and pepper.

Now, roll out your dough into thin circles. Spoon the lentil and spinach mixture onto one side of each circle, fold, and seal the edges well.

Heat oil in a deep-frying pan. Fry the samosas until they are golden brown and crispy. Ensure they are evenly cooked on all sides. Drain them on paper towels.

Serve these Lentil & Spinach Samosas hot, garnished with fresh cilantro. They are a testament to the beauty of simple, vegan cooking, offering a guilt-free way to enjoy a classic snack. Enjoy their heartiness and savor the blend of flavors and textures.

Enjoy

86. Sweet Potato & Pork Samosas

Get ready for a delightful blend of sweet and savory with these Sweet Potato & Pork Samosas. The natural sweetness of the sweet potatoes pairs exquisitely with the savory richness of pork, all encased in a light, gluten-free pastry. It's a combination that promises a dance of flavors in every bite.

Prep: 55 min. Cook: 35 min. Ready in: 1 h. 30 min. Servings: 4

Ingredients:

For the dough:

Gluten-free all-purpose flour, 2 cups

Water, as needed

A pinch of salt

Oil, about 2 tablespoons, plus more for frying

For the filling:

Sweet potatoes, boiled and mashed, 1 cup

Ground pork, cooked and drained, 1 cup

Onion, finely chopped, ¼ cup

Garlic, minced, 1 clove

Smoked paprika, ½ teaspoon

Ground cinnamon, ¼ teaspoon

Fresh sage, chopped, or dried sage, ½ teaspoon

Salt and pepper to taste

Fresh parsley, chopped, for garnish

Cooking Directions:

First, let's make the dough. In a large bowl, combine gluten-free flour and a pinch of salt. Add water gradually, kneading to form a smooth and elastic dough. Work in the oil, then set the dough aside to rest.

For the filling, in a pan, cook the onion and garlic until they're soft. Add the cooked ground pork, mixing it well with the onions and garlic. Stir in the mashed sweet potatoes, smoked paprika, cinnamon, and sage. Cook everything together until well combined and fragrant. Season with salt and pepper.

Now, roll out the dough into thin circles. Place a spoonful of the sweet potato and pork mixture on one side of each circle, fold, and seal the edges securely.

Heat oil in a deep-frying pan. Once it's hot, fry the samosas until they are golden brown and crispy. Drain them on paper towels.

Serve these Sweet Potato & Pork Samosas hot, garnished with fresh parsley. They offer a delightful mix of sweet and savory flavors, making them a perfect snack for any occasion. Enjoy the comforting warmth and the satisfying crunch that make this dish a true crowd-pleaser.

Enjoy

87. Tapiocha & Shrimp Samosas

Embark on a culinary voyage to the tropics with these Tapioca & Shrimp Samosas. Combining the delicate flavor of shrimp with the unique texture of tapioca, these samosas are a gluten-free delight, offering a burst of flavors and textures that are both refreshing and satisfying.

Prep: 60 min. Cook: 35 min. Ready in: 1 h. 35 min. Servings: 4

Ingredients:

For the dough:

Gluten-free all-purpose flour, 2 cups

Tapioca flour, ½ cup

Water, as needed

A pinch of salt

Oil, about 2 tablespoons, plus more for frying

For the filling:

Shrimp, cleaned and finely chopped, 1 cup

Coconut milk, ¼ cup

Garlic, minced, 2 cloves

Ginger, minced, 1-inch piece

Green chili, finely chopped, 1 (optional)

Fresh cilantro, chopped, ¼ cup

Lime juice, 1 tablespoon

Salt and pepper to taste

Cooking Directions:

Start by making the dough. In a bowl, mix together the gluten-free flour, tapioca flour, and salt. Gradually add water, kneading until you have a soft, smooth dough. Drizzle in the oil, give it another knead, and then let it rest.

For the filling, heat a pan and sauté the garlic, ginger, and green chili (if using) until aromatic. Add the chopped shrimp, cooking until they're pink and tender. Pour in the coconut milk, bring to a simmer, and cook until slightly thickened. Stir in the cilantro and lime juice, then season with salt and pepper.

Roll out the dough into thin circles. Place a spoonful of the shrimp mixture on one side of each circle, fold, and seal the edges well.

In a deep-frying pan, heat the oil. Fry the samosas until they are golden brown and crispy. Drain them on paper towels.

Serve these Tapioca & Shrimp Samosas hot, ideally with a tangy dipping sauce or a squeeze of fresh lime. They're a perfect blend of exotic flavors and textures, making them an excellent choice for a unique appetizer or a special snack. Dive into the taste of the tropics with each delicious bite!

Enjoy

88. Millet & Tofu Samosas

Merging the nutty flavors of millet with the versatile texture of tofu, these Millet & Tofu Samosas are a gluten-free treat that doesn't compromise on taste. They're a testament to the endless possibilities of plant-based ingredients, offering a wholesome and delicious snack option.

Prep: 55 min. Cook: 35 min. Ready in: 1 h. 30 min. Servings: 4

Ingredients:

For the dough:

Gluten-free all-purpose flour, 2 cups
Millet flour, ½ cup
Water, as needed
A pinch of salt
Oil, about 2 tablespoons, plus more for frying

For the filling:

Firm tofu, pressed and crumbled, 1 cup

Cooked millet, 1 cup

Spinach, finely chopped, ½ cup

Onion, finely chopped, ¼ cup

Garlic, minced, 2 cloves

Soy sauce, 2 tablespoons

Sesame oil, 1 teaspoon

Ground ginger, ½ teaspoon

Salt and pepper to taste

Fresh herbs (such as cilantro or parsley), chopped, for garnish

Cooking Directions:

Begin by making the dough. In a large bowl, combine gluten-free flour, millet flour, and a pinch of salt. Gradually add water, kneading until you have a smooth, elastic dough. Mix in the oil, then let the dough rest.

For the filling, heat a pan, and sauté the onions and garlic until soft. Add the crumbled tofu, cooking until slightly browned. Stir in the cooked millet and spinach, cooking until the spinach wilts. Season the mixture with soy sauce, sesame oil, and ground ginger. Adjust the salt and pepper to your taste.

Now, roll out the dough into thin circles. Spoon the millet and tofu mixture onto one half of each circle, fold, and seal the edges tightly.

Heat oil in a deep frying pan. Fry the samosas until they are golden brown and crispy, turning them occasionally for even cooking. Drain on paper towels.

Serve these Millet & Tofu Samosas hot, garnished with fresh herbs. They're a wonderful blend of healthful ingredients and savory flavors, perfect for anyone looking for a gluten-free alternative to the traditional samosa. Enjoy their unique texture and delicious taste as a snack, appetizer, or part of a meal.

Enjoy

89. Almond Flour & Berry Samosas

Bringing a sweet twist to the classic samosa, these Almond Flour & Berry Samosas combine the nutty richness of almond flour with the juicy, tangy sweetness of mixed berries. They're a delightful gluten-free dessert option, perfect for satisfying your sweet tooth in a healthier way.

Prep: 50 min. Cook: 30 min. Ready in: 1 h. 20 min. Servings: 4

Ingredients:

For the dough:

Almond flour, 2 cups

Water, as needed

A pinch of salt

Oil, about 2 tablespoons, plus more for frying

For the filling:

Mixed berries (such as strawberries, blueberries, raspberries), finely chopped, 1 cup

Sugar, 2 tablespoons (adjust based on sweetness of berries)

Lemon zest, 1 teaspoon

Cornstarch, 1 tablespoon (to thicken the filling)

Vanilla extract, ½ teaspoon

Cooking Directions:

Start with the dough. In a large bowl, mix almond flour and a pinch of salt. Gradually add water, kneading until you get a firm, pliable dough. Incorporate the oil, then let the dough rest.

For the filling, in a saucepan, combine the berries, sugar, and lemon zest. Cook over medium heat until the berries release their juices. Mix cornstarch with a little water to make a slurry, then stir it into the berry mixture. Cook until it thickens slightly. Remove from heat and stir in the vanilla extract. Let it cool before using.

Now, roll out the dough into thin circles. Place a spoonful of the berry mixture on one side of each circle, fold, and seal the edges well.

Heat oil in a frying pan. Once hot, fry the samosas until they're golden brown and crispy. Drain on paper towels.

Serve these Almond Flour & Berry Samosas warm, perhaps with a dusting of powdered sugar or a dollop of whipped cream. They're a delightful fusion of flavors and textures, offering a burst of berry goodness in every bite. Enjoy this sweet, gluten-free treat as a dessert or a special snack.

Enjoy

90. Coconut Flour & Chocolate Samosas

Indulge in the exotic flavors of these Coconut Flour & Chocolate Samosas, where the tropical essence of coconut meets the rich, decadent taste of dark chocolate. These samosas are a gluten-free, sweet delight, perfect for those who love a touch of indulgence in their treats.

Prep: 55 min. Cook: 35 min. Ready in: 1 h. 30 min. Servings: 4

Ingredients:

For the dough:

Coconut flour, 2 cups

Water, as needed

A pinch of salt

Oil, about 2 tablespoons, plus more for frying

For the filling:

Dark chocolate, chopped or in chips, 1 cup

Coconut flakes, unsweetened, ½ cup

Almond slices, ¼ cup

Sugar, 2 tablespoons (optional, adjust to taste)

Vanilla extract, ½ teaspoon

Cooking Directions:

First, let's prepare the dough. In a large bowl, combine coconut flour and a pinch of salt. Gradually add water, kneading until you have a soft, cohesive dough. Work in the oil, then let it rest, giving it time to absorb the moisture.

For the filling, mix together the chopped dark chocolate, coconut flakes, almond slices, sugar (if using), and vanilla extract. This mixture should be a harmonious blend of sweet and nutty flavors.

Now, roll out the dough into thin circles. Spoon a portion of the chocolate-coconut mixture onto one side of each circle, fold, and seal the edges well.

In a deep frying pan, heat the oil. Fry the samosas until they are golden brown and crispy. The aroma of coconut and chocolate should be tempting by now. Drain them on paper towels.

Serve these Coconut Flour & Chocolate Samosas warm. They're a fantastic dessert option, especially when paired with a scoop of ice cream or a drizzle of caramel sauce. Enjoy the delightful contrast of textures and the rich flavors that make this treat a sure hit for any sweet tooth.

Enjoy

91. Truffle & Mushroom Samosas

Indulge in a gourmet twist on the classic samosa with these Truffle & Mushroom Samosas. Combining the earthy depth of mushrooms with the luxurious aroma of truffle oil, this recipe elevates the humble samosa to a new level of sophistication. It's a true treat for the senses.

Prep: 60 min. Cook: 40 min. Ready in: 1 h. 40 min. Servings: 4

Ingredients:

For the dough:

All-purpose flour, 2 cups

Water, as needed

A pinch of salt

Oil, about 2 tablespoons, plus more for frying

For the filling:

Mushrooms (a mix of wild varieties), finely chopped, 1 cup

Truffle oil, 2 tablespoons

Garlic, minced, 1 clove

Shallot, finely chopped, 1

Fresh thyme, 1 teaspoon

Grated Parmesan cheese, ¼ cup

Salt and pepper to taste

Fresh parsley, chopped, for garnish

Cooking Directions:

Begin with the dough. In a large mixing bowl, combine the flour and salt. Gradually add water, kneading until you have a smooth dough. Work in the oil, then let the dough rest.

For the filling, heat a pan and sauté the shallot and garlic until translucent. Add the chopped mushrooms, cooking until they release their moisture and start to brown. Stir in the fresh thyme, then drizzle with truffle oil, letting its rich aroma infuse the mushrooms. Remove from the heat and mix in the grated Parmesan cheese. Season with salt and pepper.

Roll out the dough into thin circles. Place a spoonful of the mushroom and truffle mixture onto one side of each circle, fold, and seal the edges well.

Heat oil in a frying pan. Fry the samosas until golden brown and crispy, ensuring even cooking on all sides. Drain on paper towels.

Serve these Truffle & Mushroom Samosas warm, garnished with fresh parsley. They're a culinary indulgence, perfect for a special occasion or as an elegant appetizer. Enjoy the luxurious combination of flavors that make each bite a memorable experience.

Enjoy

92. Foie Gras & Red Berry Samosas

Embark on a culinary adventure with these Foie Gras & Red Berry Samosas, blending the luxurious richness of foie gras with the sweet and tart notes of red berries. This recipe is a celebration of opulent flavors, perfect for a sophisticated palate and special occasions.

Prep: 65 min. Cook: 35 min. Ready in: 1 h. 40 min. Servings: 4

Ingredients:

For the dough:

All-purpose flour, 2 cups

Water, as needed

A pinch of salt

Oil, about 2 tablespoons, plus more for frying

For the filling:

Foie gras, finely chopped, 1 cup

Red berries (like raspberries or strawberries), finely chopped, ½ cup

Shallot, finely minced, 1

Balsamic vinegar, 1 tablespoon

Thyme, a pinch

Salt and pepper to taste

Fresh arugula, for garnish

Cooking Directions:

Begin with the dough. Mix the flour and salt in a large bowl. Gradually add water, kneading until you form a smooth, pliable dough. Incorporate the oil, then let it rest.

For the filling, gently cook the shallot in a pan until soft and translucent. Add the finely chopped foie gras, cooking just until it's warmed through and starts to become tender. Stir in the red berries, balsamic vinegar, and thyme. Let the mixture simmer briefly, then remove from the heat. Season with salt and pepper.

Now, roll out the dough into thin circles. Spoon a small amount of the foie gras and berry mixture onto one side of each circle, fold over, and seal the edges securely.

In a deep-frying pan, heat the oil. Fry the samosas until they are golden brown and crispy. Drain them on paper towels.

Serve these Foie Gras & Red Berry Samosas hot, garnished with fresh arugula. They're a decadent treat, combining rich, bold flavors with a delicate balance. Perfect for a luxurious appetizer or a special treat, these samosas are sure to impress and delight your guests.

Enjoy

93. Saffron & Lobster Samosas

*Experience a touch of culinary opulence with these Saffron &
Lobster Samosas. The rich and sumptuous flavors of lobster are
beautifully complemented by the exotic aroma of saffron, creating a
samosa that's both elegant and indulgent, perfect for a sophisticated
palate.*

Prep: 70 min. Cook: 40 min. Ready in: 1 h. 50 min. Servings: 4

Ingredients:

For the dough:

All-purpose flour, 2 cups

Saffron threads, a pinch (infused in 1 tablespoon warm water)

Water, as needed

A pinch of salt

Oil, about 2 tablespoons, plus more for frying

For the filling:

Lobster meat, cooked and finely chopped, 1 cup

Garlic, minced, 1 clove

Shallot, finely chopped, 1

Heavy cream, ¼ cup

Fresh tarragon, chopped, 1 teaspoon

Lemon zest, 1 teaspoon

Salt and pepper to taste

Fresh chives, chopped, for garnish

Cooking Directions:

Begin with the dough. In a large bowl, mix the flour, salt, and the saffron-infused water. Gradually add the remaining water, kneading until you have a smooth dough. Add the oil, knead again, and let the dough rest, absorbing the saffron's golden hue and aroma.

For the filling, sauté the shallot and garlic in a pan until soft. Add the lobster meat, cooking it gently. Pour in the heavy cream, and let it simmer until slightly thickened. Stir in the tarragon and lemon zest, then season with salt and pepper.

Roll out the dough into thin circles. Place a spoonful of the lobster mixture on one side of each circle, fold, and seal the edges well.

In a deep-frying pan, heat the oil. Fry the samosas until golden brown and crispy. Drain on paper towels.

Serve these Saffron & Lobster Samosas hot, garnished with chopped chives. Each bite is a celebration of luxury and flavor, perfect for special occasions or when you're looking to impress with your culinary prowess. Enjoy the rich and refined taste that these samosas bring to your table.

Enjoy

94. Caviar & Cream Cheese Samosas

Elevate your samosa experience to a new level of luxury with these Caviar & Cream Cheese Samosas. Combining the sophisticated flavors of caviar with the smoothness of cream cheese, this recipe is a foray into haute cuisine, perfect for those who appreciate the finer things in life.

Prep: 60 min. Cook: 35 min. Ready in: 1 h. 35 min. Servings: 4

Ingredients:

For the dough:

All-purpose flour, 2 cups

Water, as needed

A pinch of salt

Oil, about 2 tablespoons, plus more for frying

For the filling:

Caviar, ½ cup

Cream cheese, softened, 1 cup

Chives, finely chopped, 2 tablespoons

Lemon zest, 1 teaspoon

Black pepper, freshly ground, to taste

Cooking Directions:

Begin by making the dough. In a large bowl, combine the flour and salt. Gradually add water, kneading to form a soft, elastic dough. Work in the oil, then let the dough rest.

For the filling, in a mixing bowl, blend the cream cheese until smooth. Gently fold in the caviar, chives, and lemon zest, being careful not to break the delicate caviar beads. Season with a touch of black pepper.

Roll out the dough into thin circles. Place a small amount of the caviar and cream cheese mixture on one side of each circle, fold, and seal the edges securely.

In a deep frying pan, heat the oil. Fry the samosas until they are golden brown and crispy. Drain on paper towels.

Serve these Caviar & Cream Cheese Samosas as a luxurious appetizer or a special treat. They're a symbol of culinary elegance and are sure to be a conversation starter at any gathering. Indulge in the lavish flavors and enjoy a moment of gourmet bliss.

Enjoy

95. Ostrich & Apricot Samosas

Venture into a culinary adventure with these Ostrich & Apricot Samosas, blending the lean, distinctive taste of ostrich meat with the sweet tanginess of apricots. This recipe is a bold fusion, perfect for those seeking to explore new and exciting flavor combinations.

Prep: 65 min. Cook: 40 min. Ready in: 1 h. 45 min. Servings: 4

Ingredients:

For the dough:

All-purpose flour, 2 cups

Water, as needed

A pinch of salt

Oil, about 2 tablespoons, plus more for frying

For the filling:

Ostrich meat, finely minced, 1 cup

Dried apricots, chopped, ½ cup

Onion, finely chopped, ¼ cup

Garlic, minced, 1 clove

Cumin, 1 teaspoon

Coriander, 1 teaspoon

Smoked paprika, ½ teaspoon

Chicken or beef broth, ¼ cup

Fresh cilantro or parsley, chopped, for garnish

Salt and pepper to taste

Cooking Directions:

Start by preparing the dough. In a large bowl, combine flour and salt. Gradually add water, kneading until you form a soft, pliable dough. Add the oil and knead again, then let the dough rest.

For the filling, sauté the onions and garlic in a pan until soft. Add the ostrich meat, cooking until it's browned. Mix in the cumin, coriander, and smoked paprika, cooking for a few minutes to release the flavors. Stir in the chopped apricots and broth, simmering until the mixture is moist but not too wet. Season with salt and pepper.

Now, roll out the dough into thin circles. Spoon a portion of the ostrich and apricot mixture onto one side of each circle, fold, and seal the edges well.

In a deep-frying pan, heat the oil. Fry the samosas until they are golden brown and crispy. Drain on paper towels.

Serve these Ostrich & Apricot Samosas hot, garnished with fresh cilantro or parsley. They're an exploration of taste, combining exotic meats with sweet fruits, wrapped in a crispy pastry. Perfect for a special occasion or as a gourmet snack, these samosas are sure to intrigue and delight your palate.

Enjoy

96. Venison & Cranberry Samosas

Embrace the rustic and rich flavors of the forest with these Venison & Cranberry Samosas. This recipe combines the lean, earthy taste of venison with the tart sweetness of cranberries, creating a samosa that's bursting with flavor and perfect for game enthusiasts and adventurous eaters alike.

Prep: 70 min. Cook: 40 min. Ready in: 1 h. 50 min. Servings: 4

Ingredients:

For the dough:

All-purpose flour, 2 cups

Water, as needed

A pinch of salt

Oil, about 2 tablespoons, plus more for frying

For the filling:

Ground venison, 1 cup

Dried cranberries, chopped, ½ cup

Onion, finely chopped, ¼ cup

Garlic, minced, 1 clove

Rosemary, finely chopped, 1 teaspoon

Red wine, ¼ cup (optional)

Brown sugar, 1 tablespoon

Salt and pepper to taste

Fresh thyme, for garnish

Cooking Directions:

Let's start with the dough. In a large bowl, mix together the flour and salt. Gradually add water, kneading to form a smooth dough. Work in the oil, then let the dough rest.

For the filling, cook the onion and garlic in a pan until they're soft. Add the ground venison, cooking until well browned. Mix in the cranberries, rosemary, and red wine (if using), letting the alcohol cook off and the flavors meld. Stir in the brown sugar, and season with salt and pepper. Let the mixture cool slightly.

Now, roll out the dough into thin circles. Spoon the venison and cranberry mixture onto one side of each circle, fold, and seal the edges tightly.

Heat oil in a deep frying pan. Fry the samosas until they are golden brown and crispy. Drain on paper towels.

Serve these Venison & Cranberry Samosas hot, garnished with fresh thyme. They offer a delightful combination of savory and sweet, wrapped in a crisp pastry shell. Perfect for a hearty snack or an unconventional appetizer, these samosas are sure to be a memorable part of any meal.

Enjoy

97. Pheasant & Pear Samosas

Step into a world of elegant flavors with these Pheasant & Pear Samosas. The combination of delicate pheasant meat with the sweet, subtle crispness of pear creates a filling that's both sophisticated and satisfying, offering a unique twist on the traditional samosa.

Prep: 65 min. Cook: 40 min. Ready in: 1 h. 45 min. Servings: 4

Ingredients:

For the dough:

All-purpose flour, 2 cups

Water, as needed

A pinch of salt

Oil, about 2 tablespoons, plus more for frying

For the filling:

Pheasant breast, cooked and finely chopped, 1 cup

Pear, finely diced, ½ cup

Onion, finely chopped, ¼ cup

Garlic, minced, 1 clove

Sage, finely chopped, 1 teaspoon

White wine, ¼ cup (optional)

Brown sugar, 1 tablespoon

Salt and pepper to taste

Fresh parsley, for garnish

Cooking Directions:

First, prepare the dough. In a bowl, combine the flour and salt. Add water gradually, kneading to form a smooth dough. Incorporate the oil, then let the dough rest, allowing the gluten to relax.

For the filling, sauté the onions and garlic in a pan until they're soft and fragrant. Add the chopped pheasant meat, cooking it gently. Mix in the diced pear, sage, and white wine (if using), letting the mixture simmer until the flavors are well combined and the liquid has reduced. Stir in the brown sugar, and season with salt and pepper.

Now, roll out the dough into thin circles. Spoon a portion of the pheasant and pear mixture onto one side of each circle, fold, and seal the edges well.

In a deep-frying pan, heat the oil. Fry the samosas until they are golden brown and crispy. Drain on paper towels.

Serve these Pheasant & Pear Samosas hot, garnished with fresh parsley. They're a perfect blend of game meat and fruit, offering a unique and upscale flavor profile. Ideal for a special occasion or as an elegant appetizer, these samosas are sure to impress and delight your guests.

Enjoy

98. Quail & Grape Samosas

Step into a culinary fairytale with these Quail & Grape Samosas. The delicate, gamey flavor of quail pairs beautifully with the sweet juiciness of grapes, creating a filling that's both refined and playful. These samosas are a wonderful fusion of flavors, perfect for those who love a touch of elegance in their meals.

Prep: 70 min. Cook: 40 min. Ready in: 1 h. 50 min. Servings: 4

Ingredients:

For the dough:

All-purpose flour, 2 cups

Water, as needed

A pinch of salt

Oil, about 2 tablespoons, plus more for frying

For the filling:

Quail meat, cooked and finely chopped, 1 cup

Grapes, seedless and halved, ½ cup

Onion, finely chopped, ¼ cup

Garlic, minced, 1 clove

Thyme, finely chopped, 1 teaspoon

Balsamic vinegar, 1 tablespoon

Brown sugar, 1 teaspoon

Salt and pepper to taste

Fresh rocket (arugula) or basil, for garnish

Cooking Directions:

Begin with the dough. In a large bowl, mix together the flour and salt. Gradually add water, kneading until you get a soft, elastic dough. Add the oil, give it one last knead, and then let it rest.

For the filling, sauté the onion and garlic in a pan until translucent. Add the finely chopped quail meat, cooking it gently. Mix in the halved grapes, thyme, balsamic vinegar, and brown sugar. Let the mixture simmer until it's rich and flavorful. Season with salt and pepper.

Now, roll out the dough into thin circles. Place a spoonful of the quail and grape mixture onto one half of each circle, fold, and seal the edges tightly.

Heat oil in a deep-frying pan. Fry the samosas until they are golden brown and crispy. Drain on paper towels.

Serve these Quail & Grape Samosas hot, garnished with fresh rocket or basil. They're a delightful combination of sophisticated and whimsical flavors, making them a perfect choice for a special occasion or as an impressive appetizer. Enjoy the delicate balance of tastes and textures in each bite.

Enjoy

99. Kangaroo & Barbecue Samosas

Dive into the bold and exotic flavors of Australia with these Kangaroo & Barbecue Samosas. Kangaroo meat is known for its lean texture and rich taste, which pairs exceptionally well with the smoky sweetness of barbecue sauce. This recipe is a daring culinary adventure, perfect for those looking to explore unique and robust flavors.

Prep: 65 min. Cook: 40 min. Ready in: 1 h. 45 min. Servings: 4

Ingredients:

For the dough:

All-purpose flour, 2 cups

Water, as needed

A pinch of salt

Oil, about 2 tablespoons, plus more for frying

For the filling:

Kangaroo meat, finely minced, 1 cup

Barbecue sauce, ¼ cup

Onion, finely chopped, ¼ cup

Garlic, minced, 1 clove

Smoked paprika, ½ teaspoon

Brown sugar, 1 tablespoon

Salt and pepper to taste

Fresh cilantro or parsley, chopped, for garnish

Cooking Directions:

First, prepare the dough. In a large mixing bowl, combine the flour and salt. Gradually add water, kneading until you have a smooth, pliable dough. Work in the oil, then let it rest.

For the filling, cook the onion and garlic in a pan until they're soft. Add the kangaroo meat, cooking until well browned. Stir in the barbecue sauce, smoked paprika, and brown sugar. Let it simmer until the mixture is moist but not too wet. Season with salt and pepper.

Roll out the dough into thin circles. Place a spoonful of the kangaroo mixture onto one side of each circle, fold, and seal the edges well.

Heat oil in a deep frying pan. Fry the samosas until they are golden brown and crispy. Drain on paper towels.

Serve these Kangaroo & Barbecue Samosas hot, garnished with fresh cilantro or parsley. They're a perfect combination of the wild and the familiar, offering a taste experience that's both unique and satisfying. Whether for a special occasion or as an adventurous snack, these samosas are sure to be a memorable treat.

Enjoy

100. Alligator & Cajun Spice Samosas

Step into the wild side with these Alligator & Cajun Spice Samosas. Alligator meat, known for its unique flavor and tender texture, is perfectly complemented by the robust and spicy Cajun seasoning. This recipe offers a taste of Southern Americana, bringing a daring and delicious twist to the traditional samosa.

Prep: 70 min. Cook: 40 min. Ready in: 1 h. 50 min. Servings: 4

Ingredients:

For the dough:

All-purpose flour, 2 cups

Water, as needed

A pinch of salt

Oil, about 2 tablespoons, plus more for frying

For the filling:

Alligator meat, finely chopped, 1 cup

Cajun seasoning, 2 teaspoons

Bell pepper, finely chopped, ¼ cup

Onion, finely chopped, ¼ cup

Celery, finely chopped, ¼ cup

Garlic, minced, 1 clove

Tomato paste, 1 tablespoon

Chicken or vegetable broth, ¼ cup

Salt and pepper to taste

Fresh thyme, for garnish

Cooking Directions:

Start by making the dough. In a large bowl, mix together the flour and salt. Slowly add water, kneading until you get a smooth and pliable dough. Work in the oil, then let the dough rest.

For the filling, heat a pan and sauté the onion, bell pepper, celery, and garlic until they start to soften. Add the chopped alligator meat, cooking until it's no longer pink. Sprinkle in the Cajun seasoning, stirring well. Add the tomato paste and broth, and let the mixture simmer until thickened. Season with salt and pepper.

Roll out the dough into thin circles. Spoon the alligator filling onto one side of each circle, fold over, and seal the edges tightly.

In a deep-frying pan, heat the oil. Fry the samosas until they are golden brown and crispy. Drain on paper towels.

Serve these Alligator & Cajun Spice Samosas hot, garnished with fresh thyme. They're a bold fusion of Louisiana flavors with the classic Indian snack, perfect for adventurous eaters and anyone looking to try something new and exciting. Enjoy this culinary escapade!

Enjoy

<u>Bonus recipes for Samosa dough</u>

1. Traditional Samosa Dough

Ingredients:
All-purpose flour, 2 cups
Carom seeds (Ajwain), 1 teaspoon
Salt, 1 teaspoon
Ghee or oil, 4 tablespoons
Water, as needed

Preparation Time: 15 minutes
Resting Time: 30 minutes
Ready In: 45 minutes

Instructions:
Mix flour, carom seeds, and salt in a bowl.
Add ghee or oil and rub it into the flour until the mixture resembles coarse breadcrumbs.
Gradually add water, kneading into a firm dough. Cover and set aside for 30 minutes.

2. Gluten-Free Samosa Dough

Ingredients:
Gluten-free all-purpose flour, 2 cups
Xanthan gum, 1 teaspoon (if your flour mix doesn't include it)
Salt, 1 teaspoon
Oil, 4 tablespoons
Water, as needed

Preparation Time: 15 minutes
Resting Time: 30 minutes
Ready In: 45 minutes

Instructions:
Combine the flour, xanthan gum (if using), and salt.
Add oil and mix well.
Gradually add water, kneading to a smooth dough. Let it rest for 30 minutes.

3. Flaky Samosa Dough

Ingredients:
All-purpose flour, 2 cups
Salt, 1 teaspoon
Butter, 5 tablespoons, cold and cubed
Ice water, as needed

Preparation Time: 20 minutes
Resting Time: 30 minutes (in the refrigerator)
Ready In: 50 minutes

Instructions:
Combine flour and salt in a bowl.
Add the cold, cubed butter and rub into the flour until you get a crumbly texture.
Gradually add ice water, kneading gently until a dough forms.
Refrigerate for 30 minutes before using.

4. Whole Wheat Samosa Dough

Ingredients:
Whole wheat flour (Atta), 2 cups
Salt, 1 teaspoon
Oil, 4 tablespoons
Water, as needed

Preparation Time: 15 minutes
Resting Time: 30 minutes
Ready In: 45 minutes

Instructions:
Mix whole wheat flour and salt.
Add oil and incorporate it well into the flour.
Slowly add water, kneading into a pliable dough. Rest for 30 minutes.

5. Spiced Samosa Dough

Ingredients:
All-purpose flour, 2 cups
Cumin seeds, 1 teaspoon
Salt, 1 teaspoon
Ghee or oil, 4 tablespoons
Warm water, as needed

Preparation Time: 15 minutes
Resting Time: 30 minutes
Ready In: 45 minutes

Instructions:
Mix flour, cumin seeds, and salt.
Add ghee or oil and mix well.
Gradually add warm water, kneading into a firm dough. Let it rest for 30 minutes.

Each of these dough recipes can be rolled out and filled with your choice of samosa filling, offering a variety of textures and flavors to suit different tastes and dietary requirements. Enjoy experimenting with these doughs for your samosa creations!

Review Request

Thank you for purchasing
Top 100 Most Delicious Samosa Recipes.

We hope you found the recipes as tasteful and delicious as we do.

Please show your support and love for samosas by leaving a review, if the recipes were delicious

Make sure to check out all the other delicious recipes in the Top 100 Most Delicious cookbook series.